HUMAN NATURE AND HISTORY

HUMAN NATURE
AND HISTORY
A RESPONSE TO
SOCIOBIOLOGY

Kenneth Bock

Columbia University Press
New York

Library of Congress Cataloging in Publication Data

Bock, Kenneth Elliott, 1916–
    Human nature and history.

    Includes bibliographical references and index.
    1. Ethnology—Philosophy.   2. Culture.   3. Socio-
biology.   4. Social history.   I. Title.
GN345.B62   306   80-15217
ISBN 0-231-05078-X (cloth)
ISBN 0-231-05079-8 (paper)

Columbia University Press
New York   Guildford, Surrey

For Margaret Hall Bock

CONTENTS

PREFACE

The central argument of this book is that explication of social and cultural differences is a primary task of the human sciences and that such explication is best sought in comparison of human histories, not in human biology or comparative ethology.

In the course of defending the integrity of human social and cultural studies I have found it necessary to give reasons for not following the frequently made suggestion that we base our enterprise on Darwinian foundations. That has involved an examination and analysis of some aspects of Charles Darwin's work. I have tried to limit my criticisms to ventures by Darwin into areas of traditional humanistic concern. I have no interest in, or qualification for, attacking Darwin's theory of descent with modification; nor is it my purpose to impugn the scholarship and genius that produced the theory.

Similarities between current sociobiology and the work of Sigmund Freud are evident, although the connection is not always acknowledged. My avoidance of the question here results from a wish to achieve sharper focus on specific arguments of the new biology. Sociobiology interprets human society as a function of human biology; Freudian psychoanalytic theory is a towering, and perhaps more complicated, structure within the same genre of interpretation.

I have sometimes used the terms *humanist* and *humanistic* to refer to students of human societies and cultures and to their scholarly concerns. Traditionally, these words have designated a particular group of Renaissance or classical scholars, especially Latinists. The *Oxford English Dictionary*, however, offers as a first definition of humanist: "A student of human affairs, or of human nature." It is in that broad sense that I use the word to indicate the distinctive interests of those who study the social and cultural life of humankind.

My intellectual debts are revealed generally in the notes. I wish to acknowledge individually, however, the generous aid given by readers of the manuscript in one or another of its stages: John Howland Rowe, Robert Nisbet, Carl E. Bock, Julia Chase, Arthur L. Caplan, Joseph G. Jorgensen, John M. Johnson, Jorge Chapa, Andrew Treno, and Jeffrey Johnson. Their criticisms and suggestions have been most helpful.

I owe special thanks to M. Katherine Mooney. Her scholarly contribution to the book has been much more on the order of collaboration than assistance.

This work has been supported by funds made available through the Committee on Research of the University of California at Berkeley.

HUMAN NATURE AND HISTORY

INTRODUCTION

Recent efforts of biologists to provide new guides for the study of human social life afford an opportunity, and perhaps create a necessity, for restating and confirming the aims of social scientific inquiry so as to specify the ways in which they resemble and differ from those of sociobiology. The various sciences of society and culture do not, of course, share a unified approach, so in the following book it will be necessary to deal with only the broadest aspects of humanistic studies as such, and with some of the particulars of comparative historical work within that genre. Choice of materials is based in part on promoting understanding between biologists and social scientists, and even on suggesting questions of possible common concern, but the principal object is to isolate distinctive concerns of students of human societies and cultures, and attention is therefore directed mainly to characteristic marks of humanistic inquiry.

This search for a humanistic identity in both method and subject matter need be motivated neither by conceit about human worth nor by academic jealousy over threatened preserves. If we are not to lose the substance of human histories as a guide to action, it is necessary that such experience be kept conceptually intact and not discarded as a mere manifestation of alleged underlying forces. Even the soothing eclecticism in which both biology and culture, and their interaction, are recognized as factors in human history is commonly marked by an ambiguity in which the question is begged, and "ultimate" determination of things is vested in the supposedly tougher realities of organic control. The human historical perspective is a fragile and perishable thing. It has been abandoned again and again in a search for immutable forces that lie behind the bewildering complexity of events that make up the lives of peoples. The attempt to locate such forces in genes is only the most recent among repeated circumventions of historical empiricism.

Broadly considered, efforts to uncover history-producing forces have focused commonly on a container called human nature. Since history, on the face of it, is the doings of human beings, it has seemed reasonable to make sense of it by discovering springs to action in human beings themselves. History thus becomes an expression of human nature, and the more we know about the evolution and structure of that nature the more, it is said, we will understand what history is all about. This is the form of the current sociobiological argument, and it will be useful to examine this sort of human-nature theory in the light of some of its long history.

It is a curious thing that the contemporary analysis of human nature as a product of organic evolution is closely associated with recent remarkable advances in the observation and evolutionary interpretation of the behavior of other animals. In light of this circumstance, some biologists regard the reluctance of social scientists to join in the "new synthesis" of sociobiology as a failure to see, or to accept, a kinship of human beings and animals in the similar organic foundations of their social lives. The failure is attributed to lack of knowledge and to moral and spiritual aversion to seeing ourselves as brutes. There is reason to recall, therefore, that man has long been regarded, in the humanistic tradition, as an animal, and that a fairly careful comparison of humans and other animals has played an important part in shaping present conceptions of human society and human culture as historical phenomena (chapter 1).

The new biology of human society has also been molded in an atmosphere of enthusiastic celebration of the hundredth anniversary of the publication of Charles Darwin's *The Origin of Species*. Darwin has been presented as having set down guidelines for a real science of human social life, and social theorists have been reprimanded for their failure to see and follow the light. The time seems past due, then, for suggesting that Darwin offered no new perspective for the humanistic disciplines, and that he supported, instead, some misleading notions that they have struggled to escape in his time and since (chapter 2).

It should be understood that the special outlook of sociobiology appears, to humanists, as only one more form of a strategy to look for explanations of human social and cultural experience outside of that experience itself. The theory of natural selection has not, so far, been used in research into human historical activities so as to yield testable results. The speculative nature of such a venture is apparent, and social scientists are understandably wary of it (chapter 3).

It is in the failure of sociobiology, and of other biological approaches, to deal with the problem of cultural differences, however, that a major barrier between the life and the social sciences is raised. If we are to explain human social and cultural phenomena in terms of an evolved human nature, then we are left with no explanation of different societies and cultures in the present or of changing societies and cultures during historical time when evolutionary changes in human beings were slight. Replies of sociobiologists to this dilemma are that (1) the differences are unimportant, (2) there might be some genetic differences that explain the cultural diversity, or (3) such minor differences are to be regarded as adaptations to various environments. The first solution is by far the most common, and it amounts to denying any significant subject matter to anthropology and sociology (chapter 4).

Despite a recent emphasis in sociocultural sciences on system problems of structure and function, and although in the long reign of social evolutionism social and cultural differences have not been regarded as theoretically significant, there is also a strong tradition in humanistic studies of explaining the various activities of humankind by their various histories. This means looking on the actions of people as real and effective producers of the diverse activities that constitute their social and cultural lives—that make up what we call a society and a culture. It involves associating the events of human actions with particular conditions, both physical and sociocultural. It means accepting and working with the idea that, in a very real sense, peoples make their own histories, whether they like it or not, and that this is what distinguishes them from other animals (chapter 5).

From such a point of view, then, we can see that

humans are not simply gregarious animals. Their societies are not like other animal societies because human
societies are products of human historical activities. Animal societies are products of natural selection. Human
society and human culture are *sui generis* and real, inasmuch as human societies and cultures have their effective source in human time and place actions. By seeing
human society and culture as possessing reality only in
the different historical instances of societies and cultures, we are able to avoid the problem of reifying Society and Culture. We are also rescued from the hol-
lowness of reducing history to biological events and so
losing touch with the very stuff of human life (chapter 6).

For the purpose of distinguishing human historical experience from human organic evolution and from the
evolutionary histories of other animals, we can contrast
activity and behavior. When humans and other animals
do things that are immediate and direct results of genetic
or other organic controls, that is behavior. It is obviously
very difficult to separate and weigh, even in nonhumans,
what we would designate firm biological controls of behavior as against a variety of environmental influences
and even tradition. And in the case of humans, controversy has gone on since at least the eighteenth century
over the shares to be given to "human nature" and to
tradition in accounting for regularly observed behavior.
Apart from these special problems, however, there are
times when human beings act in ways not prescribed by
either biological or traditional controls. We know of
these activities by virtue of their not having been present
in the given society before, and because they are unlike
the activities of people in other societies. Activity in this
sense is novel, and its novelty is not accountable in evo-

lutionary terms except in such a remote way as to lack the specificity of explanation (chapter 7).

The general argument of this book is that the historical experience of human beings in their social and cultural lives is not simply an expression of their nature. History is something in itself. To whatever extent other animals might have histories, it is obviously much more the case with man. This is the feature of human existence that is the focus of humanistic inquiry. Whatever light biology might come to shed on humanity, it would be tragic if the historical dimension of human life were left unstudied.

There is grandeur in the view that a continuity exists in nature, enabling us to see the social as a category with a variety of manifestations in the different species, to account for various results in terms of a universal process of natural selection acting in different environments, and to discern a solid basis for all of this in tangible biological materials. One leaps at the possibility of escape from an uneasy feeling that there might be such a complication of events in human experience as to defy comprehension, and yields to the hope that even if the area of chance and contingency is great, a firm and understandable system of guides and controls assures a remaining order that we can grasp and rely on. To social scientists, who work in what is actually the oldest line of inquiry, and whose labors have brought forth so little verified knowledge, the temptation to seize this promising clue is strong. But we have yielded to this temptation too often, and with barren results. The human sciences must not abandon their proper subject matter, the histories of peoples.

CHAPTER 1

ANIMALS AND MEN

There is a long history of efforts to learn about humans by comparing them with animals, and again today students of animal social behavior urge their colleagues in the study of human social behavior to join in what is represented as a common enterprise.[1]

The reluctance of most humanists to accept this invitation is not generally understood by biologists. The misunderstanding commonly consists in supposing that sociologists and anthropologists, for example, cannot accept man as an animal because that offends their pride in humanity, threatens their confidence in free will, or circumscribes their visions of a utopia shaped by a human nature for which anything is possible. Darwin warned us about pride in our species and taught us that we should seek the foundations of our cherished morality in "instinct" rather than in "God-implanted conscience." And now Konrad Lorenz pleads with us to shun vanity, to accept with humility our place in nature with other animals, and to forego the illusion that, by proper education, "all men can be turned into angelically ideal citizens."[2] The intended lesson is that social scientists fail to take a candid view of man and cling, instead, to an Enlightenment faith in his reason, his goodness, and his capacity for infinite progress.

It is difficult to understand how anyone could perceive this as the prevailing image of human nature within the generally misanthropic fraternity of social scientists. But beyond this, it should be apparent to Lorenz, as it must be to fellow writers like Desmond Morris and Robert Ardrey,[3] that people generally—or at least the book-buying public—are quite receptive to the idea that they are animals, and not very good ones. Before a rapprochement between biologists and humanists can be expected, it must be understood that the apparent coolness of the latter toward a general ethology based on the genetics of behavior does not derive from some mystical conception of a divine spark in humanity, nor from a fear of forsaking godlike powers of self-direction, nor from a revulsion against admitting a common ancestry with apes.

It is curious that many biologists today, as in Darwin's time, feel so strongly that they are delivering a repugnant message when they assert human kinship with other organisms. Perhaps the implications of the idea are more striking for biologists, and therefore more difficult to accept, and so they impute to others a similar reaction. In any event, if an understanding of the actual grounds for a humanistic distrust of the new biology is to be achieved, it is apparently necessary to lay to rest the belief that it results from a failure to accept man as an animal. That can be achieved, at least in part, by recalling that the idea of a close relationship between human and other animals lies deep in the European intellectual heritage.

It is an integral part of the Western tradition to designate humans as animals, to recognize an absolute continuity in all nature, to seek information about human beings by observing animals, to find moral guidance in the example of animals, and to accept—indeed to treasure—the idea that humans are in many ways inferior to animals.

When Darwin observed that "organic beings have been found to resemble each other in descending degrees, so that they can be classed in groups under groups,"[4] he expressed a long established view. Aristotle had put it thus:

Nature proceeds little by little from things lifeless to animal life in such a way that it is impossible to determine the exact line of demarcation, nor on which side thereof an intermediate form should lie.

Aristotle also made it clear that gradualism was characteristic of both form or structure and of "habits of life," including sociability.[5] "Continuous gradation" in nature dictated, of course, that humans be included routinely in all of Aristotle's works on animals; the point is not discussed. When he spoke of man as a political animal,[6] the meaning is clear: his nature is political and it is the nature of an animal. Aristotle saw nothing debasing in this picture of man. Just as Thomas Huxley was later to observe that no derogation of a person is suggested by recognizing that he was once a common egg, Aristotle said:

If . . . there is anyone who holds that the study of the animals is an unworthy pursuit, he ought to go further and hold the same opinion about the study of himself, for it is not possible without considerable disgust to look upon the blood, flesh,

9

bones, blood-vessels, and suchlike parts of which the human body is constructed.[7]

Given this conception of the natural spectrum, it is not surprising that Pliny, for example, was full of descriptions of human beings who resemble wild beasts, or that there was a proclivity among ancient and medieval writers to invent intermediate forms when the continuity of the organic chain was threatened by gaps in the actual materials at hand. Sexual intercourse between man and animals was taken for granted; even Saint Augustine testified to the reality of *similitudines homines*, the results of such unions. Baboons and apes, wild men (*Homo sylvestris*) and savages, were believed to stand in close relationship. In the thirteenth century, Albertus Magnus described a group of manlike creatures, such as pygmies and apes, that form a link between man and other animals.[8]

While it is true that medieval thinkers were likely to insist on the distinctness of all species, including man, the idea of a great and continuous chain of being survived as a basic orientation to nature. Given the omnipotence of God, it followed that the universe must be absolutely filled with every imaginable kind of thing and creature, and that meant that there could be no significant gap in the chain, at least not until the steps from man to angels and angels to God were reached.[9] The chain at this time was, of course, a static thing, each link a separate creation of God's. The distinction between a finely graduated spatial series and gradations in a time series representing change must always be made, if early schemes of classification are not to be mistaken for anticipations of evolutionary theory. Nonetheless, there is, even in medieval thought, a marked habit of viewing each work of God in its relation to others, and man is no exception.

The medieval conception of wild men presents an interesting problem in this regard, as well as a perspective from which to view our continuing inclination to find animal qualities in humans and to sight Big Foot or the Abominable Snowman in remote places. In the Middle Ages, wild men were imaginary creatures, compounds of human and animal traits. They were usually naked except for hair or fur, and they often carried a club or mace. Both sexes were represented.[10] In Bernheimer's judgment, wild men were created as symbols of what was detested and what was admired and longed for, representations of a psychic force like Freud's concept of the id. They were free as beasts and behaved in many ways like beasts, but were given, in the late Middle Ages, a nobility and power that excelled ordinary man's. As the life of the aristocracy lost its sheen with the rising power of the cities, and the ideals of knighthood gave way to mere form, it became fashionable to pretend to wildness and to repudiate civilization. In this respect people were using a totally imaginary being in a way they have habitually used animals and savages—to fabricate qualities in themselves from characteristics identified in others. It is clear enough, when we view this practice among medieval Europeans, that the qualities all derive from self-conceptions. The extent to which that is true for modern observations of animals is more difficult to judge, but some ethologists are certainly aware of the danger.

More pervasive than a simple comparison of animals and men, or of men and imaginary creatures, has been the strong inclination to see levels of correspondence in nature, particularly in the form of macrocosms and microcosms.[11] The procedure, common in ancient and medieval as well as in modern speculation, has been to identify similarities in distinct parts of the world that vary in size and location, so as to suggest that an entity at one level imitates or copies a corresponding thing at another level. A favorite analogy of this sort has been drawn between man as microcosm, a little world, and the great world or cosmos as macrocosm. An old form of the idea is the comparison, made by Saint Augustine as by Herbert Spencer, of the intellectual growth of an individual man and the intellectual history of the human race. The picture of ontogeny recapitulating phylogeny is another familiar instance. The persistent analogy made between the state or society and an organism—a Leviathan—reveals the same kind of thinking. Efforts to represent an organism as a society, or an environment as a community, involve a simple reversal of that analogy.[12]

Where man is taken as a microcosm the implication is that he is not just a part of nature but that he partakes of all nature, contains within himself all the features of a broadly conceived macrocosm. He is both angel and animal. He contains all the elements, all the plants and minerals. He is both weak and strong, gentle and fierce, good and evil. Sir Walter Raleigh, in 1614, gave elegant expression to the idea.

Man thus compounded and formed by God, was an abstract or modell, or briefe Storie of the Universall . . . the last and most excellent of his Creatures. . . . And whereas God created three sorts of living nature, (to wit) Angelicall, Rationall, and Brutall . . . he vouchsafed unto Man, both the intellectuall of Angels, the sensitive of Beasts, and the proper rationall belonging unto man . . . and because in the little frame of mans body there is a representation of the Universall . . . therefore was man called *Microcosmos*, or the little World.[13]

The search for "man's place in nature"—indeed, for his place in the more broadly conceived scale of being or hierarchy of souls—was also a central concern of the Elizabethans. As Eustace Tillyard reminds us, Shakespeare repeatedly compared man and beast in order to understand and portray man better. He revived the Pythagorean image of man: sometimes godlike, sometimes bestial. Man was repository of all the elements of nature, each of them weaker in him than its counterpart at another level: rational, energetic, and viable, but less rational than God, less energetic than other animals, less viable than plants. If Prospero displays the finest qualities of man and Caliban is nearly beast, still, on comparison, Prospero must recognize the animal in himself.[14]

If it is not altogether clear whether Caliban be beast or savage, that is not surprising; for Renaissance Europeans were troubled in their classification of apes, wild men, and the dark-skinned natives they had found beyond the seas. The medieval conviction that manlike creatures occupy a place in the scale between man proper and all the other animals had been supported by vague reference to pygmies or apes. It was only in the seventeenth century that more definite information on both nonhuman primates and savages opened the way for a flood of new comparisons and speculations on man's relationship to animals.

Edward Tyson's work on the "Orang Outang" is a revealing example of this abiding interest. Tyson, a skilled observer and anatomist, obtained, in 1699, the corpse of an apparently well-preserved juvenile chimpanzee, which he examined and dissected with great care. He presented his findings in a handsome volume distinguished by excellent drawings. As we would expect, Tyson's principal concern was to fix the place of his orang in the great scale of nature, and particularly to determine its relation to man. "I have made a *Comparative* Survey of this *Animal*," he wrote, "with a *Monkey*, an *Ape*, and a *Man*." [15] He was aware that he worked in a tradition. The ancients, he observed, were inclined to regard brutes as men. Now, "the *Humour* is, to make *Men* but meer *Brutes* and *Matter*." Tyson returned to the balanced judgment that man is part brute and part angel "and is that *Link* in the *Creation*, that joyns them both together." [16] The orang, he decided, was a brute, but it resembled man more than any other animal did and should be regarded, therefore, as an intermediate link between an ape and a man.[17]

. . . from Minerals, to Plants; from Plants, to Animals; and from Animals, to Men; the Transition is so gradual that there appears a very great Similitude as well between the meanest Plant, and some Minerals; as between the lowest Rank of Men, and the highest kind of Animals. The Animal of which I have given the Anatomy, coming nearest to Mankind; seems the Nexus of the Animal and Rational, as your Lordship [Tyson's patron], and those of your High Rank and Order for Knowledge and Wisdom, approaching nearest to that kind of Beings which is next above us; Connect the Visible, and Invisible World.[18]

If there is only a hint in this that there are *kinds* of men in the chain of being, the point had been made explicitly by Sir William Petty in 1677. What occupied Petty and many of his contemporaries in Europe was the search for "primitive" man's place in nature. Although the humanity of African and American natives had been questioned occasionally in the sixteenth century, the general opinion, ratified by the Church, was that mankind is one. Monsters and degenerates and manlike creatures there might be, but man proper was viewed as a single species. Petty's concern was not with pygmies and such, however. Focusing his attention on "Guiny Negros" and "Middle Europeans," he could only conclude that there were several species of man, distinguishable not only by color and outward appearance but by manners and "internall Qualities of their Minds." Petty's extension of the comparison of men and animals to a comparison of types of men was followed by various efforts in racial classification, notably Linnaeus' division of man into two species with several varieties under each.[19] The number of links in the chain increased, and the absolute continuity of the series was reenforced.

Comparison of animals and man continued with undiminished vigor and greater sophistication in the eighteenth century. A major enterprise of the Enlightenment was the description and analysis of human nature, and there was widespread agreement that this must begin with acceptance of man as an animal.[20] The object might be to uncover in this way the basic elements of human nature or to find what is distinctive about the human animal among other animals. But there can be no mistaking the fact that Enlightenment thinkers looked upon the study of human nature as a branch of *natural* philosophy. It involved the mysterious or the supernatural no more than any other branch of their inquiries.

This point can be obscured by the official existence and common acceptance at that time of a doctrine that pictured man as having been created in God's image, endowed with Godlike qualities, and provided with the means to salvation and oneness with God. Descartes had clearly delineated the qualities of the human soul that separated man from all other animals.[21] Oliver Goldsmith insisted on the distinctiveness of man's mind and soul and argued that a derivation of mind from matter is impossible.[22] And Buffon argued that the rule of imperceptible gradations in nature is broken by the distinct gap between man and monkey.[23]

But even the Cartesian distinction between man and other animals became blurred in the seventeenth and eighteenth centuries by a rejection (as in Monboddo) of Descartes' characterization of animals as mere machines. As animals came to be endowed with refinements of sense, and even a sort of reason, the gap between them and humans—especially savage or wild humans—lessened. Even Goldsmith had to acknowledge not only a remarkable similarity in physical organization between men and apes, but "some faint efforts at intellectual sagacity" in the latter.[24] The camel's nose was in the tent.

It must also be remembered that it had long been quite acceptable religious doctrine that man possessed not only divine qualities, but also all the other qualities that inhered in all other things. That covered, as we shall see, a multitude of evils. Nor should we lose sight of the fact that a basic tenet of the Christian faith represented this Godlike creature as having fallen from its high position, with dismal consequences for its immediate future. Finally, notice must be taken of the common practice among European humanists of acknowledging the divine source and support of human beings and then proceeding to say that they would discuss man as he would be bereft of such connection—"unreconstructed" man. This was sometimes presented as a separation of divine and profane history. Professor Lovejoy nicely dubbed the practice an erection of the "usual lightning-rod against ecclesiastical thunderbolts."[25]

So Rousseau, in the *Second Discourse,* acknowledged the divine source of man and then, on the pretext that he was not actually dealing in historical truths, went on to describe a quite different sort of human animal in the primitive state. Rousseau presented the classic form of the argument that the study of human society must find its basis in a portrait of human nature, and specifically in a distinction between what is original and fundamental in man and what is artificial and acquired. It would be difficult to make a clearer case than Rousseau's for the proposition that students of human society must know the natural (biological) limits within which human social behavior goes on. He argued that there is an important difference between what man is naturally and what man makes himself, and that the proper study of man deals with the former, not the latter.[26] That was a rejection of historical social and cultural processes as irrelevant, a strong reaction against Montesquieu and the historical school of thought. Rousseau could not, however, stick to this line of inquiry, for he went on to say that what really distinguished man from other animals was his "faculty of self-perfection," both as an individual and as a species.[27] This obviously is a time process, and for the process in the species (since he had dismissed actual history as misleading) Rousseau was reduced to a conjectural history.

Whatever the inconsistency in such an argument, Rousseau went on to observe that so far as original nature is concerned, there is no difference between man and animals other than the faculty of self-perfection and, possibly, man's freedom to act outside the bonds of instinct. Animals have ideas, so men and animals differ only in degree in that regard. He was ready to agree with

Montaigne that there could be a greater difference between one man and another than between a given man and a given beast.[28] Savage man began with "purely animal functions," and we should not be surprised, Rousseau observed, at finding men who closely resemble beasts. He was led to

. . . wonder whether various animals similar to men, taken by travelers for beasts without much examination, either because of a few differences they noted in exterior conformation or solely because these animals did not speak, would not in fact be true savage men whose race, dispersed in the woods in ancient times, had not had an opportunity to develop any of its potential faculties, had not acquired any degree of perfection, and was still found in the primitive state of nature.[29]

Rousseau presented a fairly detailed description of the "orangutan" and other apes and saw in these "anthropomorphic animals" some "striking conformities with the human species and lesser differences than those which could be assigned between one man and another." Because such creatures are stupid and lack speech is not good reason for denying them humanity, he maintained, for that was the condition of men in their primitive state. And it is noteworthy in this connection that Rousseau moved to a level of specificity where he rejected the notion that monkeys are a variety of man but reserved the possibility that the orangutan and pongo are. He was careful to observe, as well, that while inferences from the behavior of animals can represent man in a state of nature, this is not always the case; he doubted that men in their original state fought for possession of females, as certain animals do.[30]

So intrigued was Rousseau by the possibility that we

are related to apes that he was bold enough to suggest the ultimate experiment that could settle the matter.

There would . . . be a means by which, if the orangutan or others were of the human species, the crudest observers could even assure themselves of it by demonstration. But besides the fact that a single generation would not suffice for this experiment, it must pass as impracticable, because it would be necessary that what is only a supposition were shown to be true before the test that ought to verify the fact could be tried innocently.[31]

Rousseau's proposed experiment and his carefully hedged suggestion that apes are human were both taken up with enthusiasm by the eccentric Scot, James Burnet (Lord Monboddo). In twelve rambling and repetitious volumes,[32] this strange and original thinker demonstrates how solidly entrenched in Western thought the comparison of animals and men has been. Although he was more immediately moved by Rousseau's adventure with the orangutan, Monboddo insisted, and quite rightly, that he worked in the classical tradition of Greek and Roman philosophy.

"What is man? is a question of . . . curiosity and importance," wrote Monboddo, and in seeking an answer he turned immediately to a comparison of man and other animals. It was in the difference between man and other animals that the very foundation of a philosophy of man must be laid.[33] Man is an animal of a sort, however, and Monboddo thought "if I do not know what animal is, I cannot be said to know what man is."[34] A key difference should be noted, he observed, between men and brutes, and that difference lies in the fact that men possess a capacity for acquiring intellect whereas instinct is the gov-

erning principle of the brute. Monboddo was not completely successful in isolating intellect as a discrete
capacity and distinguishing it from sense and reason,
which he supposed brutes possess in some measure. But
man can abstract, see the species in the individual, and
be conscious of himself, and no brute has (so far) reached
such a level of mind. Because man can guide his conduct
by his intellect he can change himself in the course of
time, whereas brutes remain as they were first created.
This means that man makes himself, and there is no difference between man and brutes "except what culture
and education makes." In marking this distinction, Monboddo was anxious to dissociate himself from Locke and
Hume and others who had confounded ideas and sensa-
tions, thus denying the existence of intellect.[35]

Adamant though Monboddo was about the distinctiveness of the human species and the cultural quality of
human development, he nevertheless placed man in the
finely graduated scale of being.

> . . . man, being a little world, as the antients called him, has in
> his frame a portion of everything to be found in nature . . . .
> elements of which the inanimate world is composed . . . the
> growth and nutrition of the vegetable . . . sense, memory, and
> imagination, belonging to the animal life . . . and, last of all,
> he acquires intellect.[36]

The brute in man is part of his basic nature, even a great
part of his excellency. In his original state man was a
wild animal. We can see him still in degrees of this state
by observing savages in distant lands, savages in Europe
(wild men, that is—Monboddo drew no distinction),
idiots, infants, Peter the Wild Boy, la fille sauvage, Europeans of limited intellect, and that particularly backward
man, the orangutan. Some men have progressed out of

this state and have distinguished themselves from brutes, but the state is nevertheless a reality. Monboddo argued, in his peculiar fashion, that

wherever there is progress, there must be a beginning; and the beginning in this case can be no other than the mere animal: For in tracing back the progress, where else can we stop? If we have discovered so many links in the chain, we are at liberty to suppose the rest, and conclude, that the beginning of it must hold of that common nature which connects us with the rest of the animal creation.[37]

The linkage was tightened in Monboddo's casual consideration of the idea that brutes might be capable of benefitting from education and culture. He was moved by the ancients' opinion that brutes are capable of reason and improvement. He was ready to grant that just as man acts by instinct as well as intellect, so brutes act in some degree by intellect. This followed, again, from the principle that the universe is perfect, with "no gap or interval in it, things running into one another, like shades of different colours." Monboddo could also get specific about the brutes that might stand close to man in this regard. In one passage he placed the elephant number one in the matter of intellect, with the dog probably running second. On another occasion he thought the beaver, of all the animals not of our species, "comes the nearest to us in sagacity." Even in stressing his point that the human mind is radically different from the brute mind, Monboddo argued that therefore man can be compared only with animals of a "higher order"—dogs, horses, elephants, beavers. Monkeys, apes, and baboons he regarded as among those species "which come nearest to the human," and he reckoned them high in sagacity, though not capable of intellect.

Because Monboddo was convinced that intellect is a product of society, rather than the reverse, he was susceptible to a line of reasoning that would place the most social brutes nearest to man. Accordingly, he paid considerable attention to animal societies. His first observation was that brutes can live complex social lives without language; this supported his basic proposition that language was not necessary to human society but was instead its product. (Neither society, nor language, nor any idea—including the idea of God—was "natural" to man.) The literature on bees, ants, beavers, baubicis (a foxlike animal), seacats, wild boars, horses, and hares was examined by Monboddo with varying attention to detail. He was not seriously interested in monkeys, apes, and baboons because he thought they had never been closely united in society, but also, no doubt, because he knew practically nothing about their social life.

Monboddo came out of all this with no firm conclusions. Beavers, whom he regarded as living in the "most strict society," do not, he believed, possess anything like human intellect. On the other hand, if a social life of cooperative labor is supposed to produce language, then the possibility of beavers learning to speak cannot be ruled out. Bees and ants, despite the intricacy of their social orders, are of little interest because their behavior is purely instinctual. In general, Monboddo had to conclude that we simply do not know the extent to which brutes could improve by culture. But improvement is possible.[38]

The place of the orangutan in Monboddo's natural history has been exaggerated in commentary. He had read Tyson and, of course, Rousseau, and was an avid collector of every bit of information, rumor, and gossip about this general and vague ape form. He needed to find members of the human species who were without speech in order to buttress his general thesis that language is not natural to man. Mute wild men were apparently insufficient for his purpose, and alleged tribes of savages without language were hard to pin down. Monboddo conferred humanity on the "barbarous nation" of "Orang Outangs," and thus proved not only that speech is only a capacity in man but also that the natural state of man actually exists. His orang possessed intellect, although it was not developed, and displayed human traits of docility, decency, honor, and justice. It was capable of love and friendship. On the physical side, Monboddo accepted tales of male orangs copulating with human females, with offspring resulting, but he did not know whether the offspring were fertile. That the orang could not speak did not signify much. Nobody had bothered to teach it, and learning speech is a very difficult thing, as we know from the cases of deaf-mutes and children and wild men. Rousseau was right, Buffon wrong—the orang is human, and the difference between a savage and a civilized man is greater than the difference between an orang and a savage.[39]

But the orang was only another link in the great chain that Monboddo constructed. He stressed the point so that we may not deny our "relation" to the orang out of false pride. It would be vanity, he said, not to accept the fact that we are "of a race who were once Orang Outangs." We might as well, he went on, be ashamed of once having been an embryo.[40]

This sounds very much like Darwin and Thomas Huxley urging us, a century later, to accept our place in nature, and biologists doing the same today. It should not, however, suggest that Lord Monboddo had an idea of organic evolution anything like Darwin's.[41] Monboddo was mindful of what the sacred books said about the "origin of our species," but he, too, avoided ecclesiastical thunderbolts simply by dealing with man only after the Fall. He supposed that that calamity isolated person from person, ending society and all the human attributes associated with society, including language. Left only with the capacity to recapture his God-given attributes (he would regain only some of them on this earth), man was at that point nothing but a brute. The natural history of man that Monboddo sought to reconstruct dealt only with the period from the Fall to the present, and it was a process of growing up in which the progress of the species was strictly analogous to the progress of the individual from childhood to maturity. That some specimens of the race remained in a very backward state—the orang or the savage, for example—was a result of adventitious circumstances about which Monboddo had no historical information. It was a stroke of good fortune, as he saw it, that this situation provided him with evidence of origins and stages in the process. This is classical social or cultural evolutionism, and it resembles Darwinian theory only in its dedication to gradual progress and the delineation of stages in a time process by an arrangement of differences in the present. Monboddo was careful to point out that progress in civil society is not "from nature," for nature is "permanent and unchangeable."

And, accordingly, the wild animals, who are undoubtedly in a state of nature, still preserve the same œconomy and manner of life with no variation, except such as change of circumstances may make absolutely necessary for the preservation of the individual or the species; and the variation goes no farther than the necessity requires.[42]

It seems clear, then, that when Monboddo referred to a law of nature whereby "no species of thing is formed at once, but by steps and progression from one stage to another," he spoke of ontogeny, not phylogeny. It was the change from seed to vegetable, from embryo to animal, that he described.[43] Even in the case of man, his present capacities are the same he had "from the beginning."[44] There had been no evolution of a capacity for culture.

Lord Monboddo's assiduous, if ill-informed, comparison of animals and man in order to learn about the latter demonstrates in rather striking fashion the limitations of such an undertaking. What the comparison yielded for him is essentially the remarkable insight that human beings differ from other animals not so much by inherent superiority, or moral distinction, or "divinity," but by the fact that human beings have a history and other animals have not. Nor is the history a form or structure that stands outside or over the activities of people and shapes the content of their civilization and their destiny. Rather, it is a history in which, as Monboddo put it, man makes himself.[45] Men are to be understood, therefore, only in their coming-to-be, not in their being. Their place in nature—if that consideration is relevant at all—is not to be determined in ontological terms, not to be identified by inherent springs or guides to action, and certainly not to be fixed by "God-implanted conscience," or God-implanted anything else. Their place is to be found by an examination of their historical activities, the results of which vary from time to time and place to place.

25

Other animals, as Monboddo saw them, are creatures wound up and set to march through their specific routines, unchanging over very long periods of time. When he denied man an original nature of any particular potential, and endowed him with an original nature that is nothing but capacity for an intellect untrammeled by a fixed program of action, he declared original nature to be of no significance. Monboddo learned that a comparison of man and other animals could tell him only that that was not the way to learn about man. He still, however, had the vision of a "natural history" of man before him, and therefore went but a little distance towards a definition of the problem of cultural differences and a conception of history as plural.

Acceptance of man as an animal was, then, common in the Western Enlightenment, the Renaissance, the Middle Ages, and in antiquity. But more than that he was often seen as an ordinary, inferior, or bad animal, in danger even of losing touch with the God who was to guide him out of the pit in which the Fall had left him.

One form of the attack on human nature appeared in the idealization of animal life presented in the "happy beast" literature of the seventeenth and eighteenth centuries.[46] Although the representation of animals as morally and intellectually superior to people was often merely a literary or satirical device, it is clear that there was a genuine questioning of human superiority. Theriophily involved an expressed judgment that animal life can be edifying, that we might return to simple virtue by learning from the beasts, and that man is the only animal guilty of—or capable of—sin. If animals do not have

souls, it was argued, at least they do not carry the awful
burden of a soul alienated from God and damned by original sin. Comparison of man and animals was now not
only acceptable; the question was whether it might not
involve injustice to the brutes.

If Rousseau and Monboddo placed man in close prox-
imity to other animals, they did accept the Cartesian distinction between the human and other minds, and they
were reasonably cheerful about the possibility of the race
recovering in some measure from a state of decline. Their
judgment stands very close to Thomas Huxley's in his
discussion of man's place in nature.[47] Earlier in the century, however, a vicious blow against human nature had
been struck by Bernard Mandeville.

When Monboddo wished to defend himself against
charges of having placed man too low in the natural
scale, he would point out that he had not, at least, gone
as far as Mandeville. Mandeville responded to Lord
Shaftesbury's lofty portrait of human nature by observing
that "the Ideas he had form'd of the Goodness and Excellency of our Nature, were as romantick and chimerical
as they are beautiful and amiable."[48] After taking care to
state that he was speaking of neither Jews nor Christians,
"but meer Man, in the State of Nature and Ignorance of
the true Deity" (the usual lightning rod), Mandeville presented people as utterly selfish and completely bereft of
the virtues they claim. This is a result of inward passions
which, unknown to men, "govern their Will and direct
their Behaviour." *Appearance* of virtue in both assertion
and behavior is based upon a calculation of benefits to
self available through deceit and hypocrisy, and by these
means one class of the species has exploited the other.
All apparent virtue, he maintained, therefore has its basis

27

in private vice. Parents teach their children hypocrisy because its utility has become evident. Mandeville, like his comrades past and present in human-nature analysis, expressed fear that all this would not be gladly received by people because they hate to face the truth about themselves. But, again, he spoke with candor to man and could not see "that there is any Impiety in putting him upon his Guard against himself."[49] And his books sold well.

Later in the eighteenth century Monboddo's countryman, David Hume, developed a materialist and skeptical philosophy that once more challenged optimism about man.

The time had passed [Bryson observes] when one could assent to the dictum of Thomas Aquinas that the significant character of man was "his desire to know the truth about God and to live in communities." Man had to be seen as one of the animals, whatever else might be said of him.[50]

And he was an animal (as Adam Smith knew and Hume meant to prove) moved far more by instinct than by reason.

Hume's approach to the question has a modern ring. He noted (in 1740) that just as anatomists compare the bodies of humans and beasts, so students of mind could profitably follow a similar course. Comparison, he said, yields in the case of mind a basic similarity among animals and men in the passions and in the manner in which they arise and operate. The same "relations of ideas" exist in the minds of humans and other animals, for in both cases they are based on sensation—they have a material foundation. Pride and humility and love and hatred are the same thing in men and in animals: "There is no force of reflection or penetration required. Everything is conducted by springs and principles, which are not peculiar to man, or any one species of animals."[51]

Hume and other skeptical psychologists in the eighteenth century thus raised basic questions about the unique quality of human reason. In so doing they continued a negative view of man that had persisted since the early Renaissance. Because their views were presented in lively political discourse, Machiavelli and Hobbes have attracted the most attention in this regard. Machiavelli stripped people of all their cherished humane qualities and reduced them to the status of animals governed most effectively by force and fraud. Thomas Hobbes, while leaving man with just enough reason to come in out of the rain, made it plain that here is an animal that, so far as natural endowment is concerned, is nasty and brutish. When, however, we compare Shakespeare's Caliban with Machiavelli's man, who came a century before, and Hobbes' man, who followed by half a century, it becomes apparent that we are dealing here with what Professor Myres called "a type already widely current, and generally accepted in popular belief."[52] Whence that type?

It would be difficult to say just when man began to lose his high place in European estimates, but certainly it was long before 1859. In both medieval and modern images he was, of course, a fallen object, the heir of sin through Adam's seed. But apparently during the Renaissance an even more serious situation was envisaged for him, a situation in which his status as God's central concern, his position in the whole drama of salvation, became questionable. Theodore Spencer situates this crisis in European thought in a broad context of doubt and confusion precipitated by rational questioning of traditional pictures of order in the universe, in the institution of government, and in the series of created beings.[53] The result was a dislocation of man's place in the hierarchy of souls and a reexamination of the proportions of the various and contradictory elements in his nature. From this Renaissance controversy concerning human nature there emerged an image of man that, by comparison, makes the "naked ape" look quite respectable.

Montaigne is the central, and certainly the most engaging, figure in the dispute. Writing in about 1576, he asked us to take a close look at man alone, destitute of divine knowledge and grace (the usual nod to the Church). What we shall see, he insisted, is a "miserable and puny creature" with no discernible advantage over other animals.

To us [humans] has been allotted inconsistency, irresolution, uncertainty, sorrow, superstition, solicitude about things to come, even after we shall have ceased to live, ambition, avarice, jealousy, envy, inordinate, furious and untamable desires, war, falsehood, disloyalty, detraction and curiosity.[54]

Whatever, he wondered, could have led such wretches to suppose that they are superior to the beasts, much less the center of the universe and paramount in God's concern? It is only in our own stupidity that we consider animals stupid. Our vaunted reason is a weak faculty that leaves us unable to master even ourselves, to say nothing of nature. Our minds do not clearly grasp the little they do grasp. That is because—and here Montaigne anticipates the sensational psychologists—human knowledge has its basis in the senses, and the senses are notoriously unreliable.[55]

Montaigne drove directly at the citadel—the human soul—and bound it in a material, biological determinism. The body, he argued, has its weaknesses, and these are transferred to the mind. The feelings (passions) and emotions are strong influences on the course of both thought and action. There is no sturdy and independent force of will or of reason.

The shocks and agitations that our soul receives through the bodily passions have a great influence upon her; but still more have her own feelings, which have so strong a hold upon her, that it is perhaps tenable that she is only moved and propelled by the breath of her own winds, and that, unless stirred by them, she would remain inactive . . . it is a well-known fact that most of the noblest actions of the soul proceed from, and have need of this impulsion of the feelings.[56]

When Montaigne compared man with other animals he found that it is only our "natural and original infirmity" of presumption that blinds us to the fact that we are the frailest of all creatures living under the worst conditions of all the animals. Speech does not distinguish us, for other animals communicate in what is perhaps a more universal system of signs and gestures. In the arts, we are excelled by the bees, the birds, and the spiders, and we have no grounds for saying that their work is by instinct and ours by reason. And even if there be such a distinction, Montaigne continued, what vanity it is to suppose that it is better to act from "impulsive and fortuitous liberty" than from "natural and irresistible condition." Similarly in matters of morality or virtue, Montaigne saw animals as at least the equal of man. Animals are more beautiful than men: the apes, who most resemble us in external and facial shape, and pigs, who are most like us in inward and vital parts, are the "ugliest and meanest of

31

the whole herd." In general, though, human beings are neither superior nor inferior to other animals. There are orders and degrees, but we are all parts of the same Nature; and "Man must be forced and lined up within the barriers of this organization."[57]

Comparison convinced Montaigne that there can be a greater difference between two given men than between a given man and a given animal. And it followed that careful observation of (1) the habits of animals could be joined to our knowledge of (2) natives in foreign lands and of (3) the ancients, for the purpose of constructing a natural history that would encompass all of the past, present, and future. For, "It is one same Nature that rolls its course."[58] Thus, in the sixteenth century, Montaigne arrived, as we shall see, at a complete statement of the method that continues to be used in recovering the history of man from his animal origins to a present state.

The misanthropic image of man has been only a part of a tendency in Western thinking to see man as another animal in a natural parade that marches in close order. From this broad perspective all nature is seen as a unity, a whole composed of finely graduated parts that stand in close relation to each other along a continuum marked by levels of correspondence, at each of which universal principles operate similarly to produce analogous results. The theory of descent with modification by means of natural selection is thoroughly in keeping with that perspective, and it dramatically reenforced it by placing man in an organic instead of a broader ideal genealogy. The placing of man "in nature" did not wait upon the work of Darwin and Huxley. The belief in a great chain or scale of being was in itself sufficient basis for accepting other animals as partners in a common existence. The macrocosm-microcosm imagery similarly tied man closely not only to other animals but to all other entities in the universe. Books on "pop ethology" sell, not because they introduce such a notion to the public, but because they exploit its established presence in the public mind. It is an ingrained habit of hierarchical thinking that makes the study of animals seem relevant to the study of human history.

Questions can be raised about the seriousness of the speculations we have been examining. Certain it is that Rousseau and Monboddo often appear to be having fun with the ideas they juggle. Samuel Johnson might have been quite right in supposing that Rousseau knew himself for a fool in suggesting that the orangutan is a man. Again, the biting satire in Montaigne and Mandeville is apparent.

The ideas they were expressing, however, have been too widespread in time and place to be regarded as whimsy. Whatever their scientific quality, they are carefully worked out ideas, they have persisted for centuries, and their facets reflect many lines of thought in a variety of contexts.

The pressing question suggested by this chapter in our intellectual history is not, then, why we have refused to accept ourselves as animals, but why we have insisted on doing so, and why we have gone farther to picture ourselves as inferior animals. That must be a difficult question to answer, for if appeal is made only to evidence of concrete similarities between human and other animals, evidence of concrete differences can match it.

There is, of course, the Christian tradition of the Fall.

Montaigne and Mandeville repeatedly remind us that the poor human creature they seem to revile is, after all, not as God had created it, but actually a dehumanized version of the original Adam, almost cut off from God, and reduced to a mere glimmer of intellect encased in flesh. Comparison with the beast would seem appropriate.

The habit no doubt also reflects a strong desire to be part of a nature untamed and unsullied by the oppressive artifices of civilization. There is the conviction that we cannot live with each other as people if we cannot live with animals. And, of course, there are the obvious and compelling facts of similar physical structures and functions, extending in the case of some primates to striking resemblance.

Given the strong pull of the idea that we are animals, it is tempting to see it satisfying a deep human need. It has been suggested that the notion of man's beastliness is thus welcomed as relief from guilt feelings about our conduct; it serves in this way as a substitute for the doctrine of original sin.[59] Nicole, in 1683, turned the question of pride neatly around and offered such an explanation when he observed that

the reason why philosophers reduce men to the level of beasts is not humility, but pride, for it gives them the chance to justify their passions. By proving that men are no different from beasts, they gain authority for living like beasts.[60]

Or, as Montaigne put it with his usual succinctness, it is "safer to leave the reins of our conduct in the hands of Nature than to keep them in our own."[61]

However we account for our curious inclination to regard ourselves as being like other animals, it seems clear that we have done so for centuries and that the comparison has been used throughout Western intellectual history to shed light on the nature of man and his history. The shortcomings of humanistic inquiry cannot be blamed on our refusal to accept our place in the animal world.

CHAPTER 2

THE DARWINIAN HERITAGE

The centennial of the appearance of *The Origin of Species* initiated an enthusiastic reexamination of the implications of Darwin's suggestion that the theory of descent with modification would throw light on "the origin of man and his history."[1]

In the ensuing discussion, biologists have repeatedly advised students of human society and culture that they are hampered in their inquiries by their refusal to take Darwin's work as point of departure and as guide. Thus George Gaylord Simpson describes as "worthless" all attempts to understand human nature that appeared before 1859, and tells us that we should ignore them completely.[2] Richard Dawkins deplores the fact that the humanities are being taught today "almost as if Darwin had never lived."[3] Julian Huxley sees the "foundations provided by Darwinism" as the most promising base for a science of human history.[4] Konrad Lorenz is gratified that some anthropologists have at last grasped the inferences of Darwin's discoveries.[5] Michael Ghiselin cannot understand why sociologists and anthropologists have not applied the Darwinian hypothesis to the evolution of man and society or why they cling to social theories that were "rendered untenable in 1859."[6]

There is a note of true exasperation in such comments, a genuine incredulity that humanists had not revolutionized their inquiries when it was demonstrated that human beings had come to be in the manner of other organisms instead of being a separate and special creation in the image of God. Such a thunderous revelation would certainly seem to have called for, to say the least, a radical shift of perspective.

Yet it is quite true that investigators of human societies and cultures did not materially alter the course or content of their studies with the publication of *The Origin of Species*, or even of *The Descent of Man*, in 1871. The nineteenth-century proliferation of historical and comparative studies of human institutions and artifacts was well under way before Darwin wrote, and after 1859 the enterprise was, in fact, often carried on in conscious independence of Darwin's work.[7] Labored efforts to apply Darwinian terminology to earlier concepts of human historical processes there were, but these remained on the level of analogy and could hardly impress the evolutionary biologist then or now. When we read such giants of nineteenth-century social theory as Karl Marx, Émile Durkheim, and Max Weber we find, apart from polite kudos and an occasional turn of phrase, no real utilization of Darwinian theory.

The lack of substantial Darwinian impact on social scientists is explicable by the facts, first, that much of what Darwin had to say is not new to them, and, second, that he suggested a line of inquiry that essentially bypasses the questions they regard as central to their disciplines. If lines of communication are to be established between biologists and humanists today, these facts must be understood.

Darwin lived in a period when European thinking about time processes was profoundly affected by the idea of progress.[8] This idea, whose roots lie deep in the history of Western thought, represents the present as a product of regular change in past time. Change is characteristically pictured as similar to the growth of an individual organism: it is slow, gradual, continuous; it is immanent in the thing changing; it can be depicted as proceeding through a series of finely graduated stages or phases; it is eventless. On the premise that there are entities, things, that undergo such change in their coming-to-be, and that instances within each kind of thing come to be in the same way, it follows that all *differences* within a single kind of thing must represent degrees of coming-to-be for that thing. Closely associated with this notion of individual growth and transformation is a picture of an orderly universe in which all the kinds of things share a common mode of change with a variety of contents, establishing a cosmic continuity as unbroken as the steps in the coming-to-be of any one thing. This image was presented as a chain of being or levels of correspondence or, with a special arrangement of forms, as relations of microcosm and macrocosm.

It would have been unusual for Darwin to have escaped entirely the influence of such a pervasive and powerful idea system, and he did not. Thus:

39

Although we have no good evidence of the existence in organic beings of an innate tendency towards progressive development, yet this necessarily follows. . . . through the continued action of natural selection. For the best definition which has ever been given of a high standard of organisation, is the degree to which the parts have been specialised or differentiated; and natural selection tends towards this end, inasmuch as the parts are thus enabled to perform their functions more efficiently.[9]

In addition to this tendency toward the higher through specialization and differentiation, Darwin saw a more general progressive movement, in that "new species become superior to their predecessors; for they have to beat in the struggle for life all the older forms, with which they come into close competition." On both grounds, therefore,

modern forms ought, on the theory of natural selection, to stand higher than ancient forms. Is this the case? A large majority of palaeontologists would answer in the affirmative; and it seems that this answer must be admitted as true, though difficult of proof.[10]

He thought that we could look forward to a long future, and "as natural selection works solely by and for the good of each being, all corporeal and mental endowments will tend to progress towards perfection."[11] This is said of the history of organic forms, but Darwin expressed similar views regarding the history of human civilization. While he believed that progress was not necessary in all human tribes, just as progress was not innate in organisms, he thought nevertheless that

progress has been much more general than retrogression; that man has risen, though by slow and interrupted steps, from a lowly condition to the highest standard as yet attained by him in knowledge, morals and religion.[12]

40

He did not, of course, attempt to demonstrate the process, for he felt comfortable relying, in *The Descent of Man*, on the demonstration already made by anthropologists like Edward Burnett Tylor, John Ferguson McLennan, and Sir John Lubbock. As Darwin saw it, cultural evolutionists of his time had supplied evidence that a natural selection of more advanced tribes had been going on in human history, and that Western civilization was the result.

The idea of social and cultural development was shared by Darwin and humanists of his day, and it should be clear that Darwin received the idea from humanists, and not the reverse. It is enough to remember that a belief in the fixity of species had never been accompanied in Western thought by a belief in the fixity of human social or cultural forms. The idea of progress, of development, or of evolution in its broadest sense was applied in some detail to human culture history many centuries before it was used by Darwin's predecessors in an effort to depict the history of kinds of organisms.

The method used by Darwin to demonstrate a progress in phylogeny, or in the history of life forms, also bore striking resemblances to what Auguste Comte had called the comparative method of sociology. It is in this respect especially that nineteenth-century social scientists were unlikely to have seen new paths of inquiry revealed in *The Descent of Man*. This method consisted in the conversion of a hierarchy or classification of coexistent forms into a temporal process of successive stages. Construction of the hierarchy, or coexistent series, for Comte and his followers, depended on a prior philosophy of history and, far less significantly, on dated and archaeological evidence of actual histories. In Darwin's case the contributions made by comparative anatomy, embryology, and the fossil record made the procedure more complicated, but it looked, to humanists, to be in principle the same procedure that they had been following in historical reconstruction since the time of Thucydides.

In this conceptual operation of converting a hierarchy of forms of societies, cultures, social institutions, or cultural elements into a temporal series, special attention is paid to likenesses between contemporary non-European, tribal, nonliterate peoples and ancient peoples. Then, on the assumption that modern Europeans once passed through a historical stage like that revealed by scanty historical information about the ancients, contemporary, directly observable, savages become richer documents for the recovery of early European history. These comparisons lead easily, among investigators accustomed to hierarchical thinking, to a conviction that degrees of savagery exist and can be used to provide details of the early history of mankind in general. From there it is but a step to the proposition that all peoples existing or historically known can be taken as representatives of successive stages in a universal human history.

The presuppositions that underlie this procedure are derivations from the idea of progress. A basic assumption is that all peoples have similar culture histories, in the same way that all individual organisms of a given kind pass through similar processes of growth or development. It follows that any people at a given time (barring deviant or accidental cases) must represent a phase in culture history as such, just as any individual organism of a kind (barring pathology and accident) must represent a stage in the general growth pattern of that kind of organism. A spatial array of cultural differences does not indicate the order in which the differences must be arranged to represent a process of change through time. It is necessary, therefore, to approach these data with a general idea of the course of human history. The idea of progress serves this purpose. It pictures human culture history as a process of slow, gradual, continuous change from the simple to the complex in form and function, which carries mankind through savagery and barbarism to civilization. These criteria fail to distinguish gradations, however, and cultures are actually arranged along a continuum on the basis of their degree of similarity to European culture, which is taken to be the most advanced member of the series.

Given this tradition in the human sciences of building developmental social and cultural series, it is unlikely that nineteenth-century anthropologists and sociologists should have been impressed by the novelty of Darwin's procedures for reconstructing the manner of man's development from a preexisting form through stages leading to his highest manifestation in modern European civilization. In The Descent, Darwin builds a series which moves from ape to civilized man roughly through steps represented in its later phases by existing (1) idiots, (2) infants, (3) savages, (4) uncultivated men in civilized societies, (5) women in civilized societies, and (6) boys in civilized societies.[13] The succession is not expressly defined, nor is it presented in its totality in any one place, but the outline is clear enough. Emphasis is on connecting apes, Negroes, and civilized man by rudiments. Thus, Darwin notes that advanced man possesses an ear with a lobule; a rudiment of a lobule is found in a gorilla; in Negroes it is often absent. In European man the nictitating membrane, or third eyelid, exists as a mere rudiment; it is somewhat larger in Negroes and Australians. In many animals the sense of smell is important; it is more highly developed in dark races of men than in white and civilized races. Among civilized men, wisdom teeth are rudimentary, small, and subject to decay; in the Melanian races they are large and sound. A foramen or perforation in the humerus is occasionally present in man; it was more frequently present in ancient man; it occurs, though not constantly, in various anthropoid and other apes; it occurs frequently in the Negro. The malar bone in some of the Quadrumana normally consists of two parts; this is its condition in the human fetus at two months; through arrested development it sometimes remains thus in adult man, but "more especially in the lower prognathous races" and among ancient races. The true character of human canine teeth is indicated by the conical form of the crown; the conical form is most pronounced in the Melanian races, especially the Australian. The human foot comes to lose its prehensile power; this has been less the case among savages.[14]

In some instances, these relationships are rather finely drawn by Darwin. He notes that in microcephalous idiots the jaws are markedly prognathous, so that they resemble "the lower types of mankind." Idiots are also "curiously fond of climbing up furniture or trees;" boys delight in climbing trees. The thoughtful actions of "higher animals" and "uncultivated man" are comparable. Monkeys, microcephalous idiots, and the "barbarous" races of mankind tend to imitate whatever they hear. Savages and animals (dogs) have similar beliefs in unseen agencies. Animals sometimes expel a wounded member from the herd, or kill it; North American Indians leave the feeble behind to perish. The "barbarian" and the "uncultivated man" are incapable of higher morality. "Lower animals," "lowest savages," and "cultivated man" display a developing sense of beauty, in that order.[15] Infants and the insane exhibit parallel force in the expression of emotions; idiots snarl savagely, and snarling is probably more common among savages than among civilized races.[16] Europeans repress signs of fear more than savages; the sphincter muscles of savages are often relaxed in a state of fear, as is the case with frightened dogs and monkeys. Civilized adult males are less emotionally demonstrative than savages—they weep less; even among civilized Europeans, Englishmen rarely cry, whereas some continentals shed tears freely; Englishmen shrug their shoulders far less frequently and energetically than Frenchmen or Italians do.[17]

The savage-woman-boy-man series is succinctly presented by Darwin in this remarkable example:

a savage will risk his own life to save that of a member of the same community, but will be wholly indifferent about a stranger: a young and timid mother urged by the maternal instinct will, without a moment's hesitation, run the greatest danger for her own infant, but not for a mere fellow-creature. Nevertheless many a civilized man, or even boy, who never before risked his life for another, but full of courage and sympathy, has disregarded the instinct of self-preservation, and plunged at once into a torrent to save a drowning man, though a stranger.[18]

And perhaps Darwin's general orientation to the use of the contemporary savage as an historical document to link civilized man with lower primates is most forcibly illustrated in his observation that "The resemblance to a negro in miniature of Pithecia satanas with his jet black skin, white rolling eyeballs, and hair parted on the top of the head, is almost ludicrous."[19]

Insofar as these comparisons involved social or cultural items, Darwin was guided in his arrangement of them by prevailing opinion among anthropologists. This meant accepting European culture as the latest, highest product of human history. It involved identifying the "earliest," lowest culture in terms of the degree of its difference from European culture. And, by implication at least, it required connecting these two extremes by a continuous series of intermediate forms chosen from all known cultures. Darwin (and most of his colleagues in anthropology, for that matter) did not pay much attention to detail in these intermediate forms, and, as we have seen, instead of seeking connections in actual cultures, followed the common practice of identifying them in children, defectives, women, and the lower classes in advanced societies.

Readers of the anthropological literature of Darwin's day can hardly fail to be struck by his unqualified acceptance of this Europocentric creed. It is certainly in strong contrast to the measured caution of Edward Burnett Tylor,[20] for example, to say nothing of the many outright contemporary rejections of such views, which will be noted in later chapters. So far as Darwin was concerned, there is simply no question that the western nations of Europe stand "at the summit of civilization," and that among those nations the Anglo-Saxons excel.[21] Non-European tribal peoples, on the other hand, are savages devoid of real religion, incapable of enjoying true beauty. Judging by the "hideous ornaments, and the equally hideous music admired by most savages," Darwin could only conclude that their aesthetic faculty is less highly developed than that of birds. They are intemperate, licentious, and given to unnatural crimes, and their reasoning powers are poorly developed. Some authors, such as Lecky in his *History of European Morals,* had recently spoken favorably of savage morality; Darwin would have none of it.[22] He was insensitive to the social and cultural impact of European imperialism on the lives of other peoples and was concerned mainly with the fact that the changed conditions of life introduced by colonialism adversely affect savage fertility and health, just as changed life conditions similarly affect apes. Thus the natives of California, "reclaimed" by the missionaries, had nearly all perished, "although well treated, not driven from their native land, and kept from the use of spirits." Extinction following competition of tribe with tribe and race with race is to be expected.[23]

It should be noted that while Darwin was not engaged in the same enterprise that occupied most social and cultural developmentalists,[24] he was in complete agreement with them not only about the continuity of change in the abstract, but also about the continuity of the coexistent series of social and cultural forms. Just as developmentalists had argued since at least the eighteenth century that every nuance of savagery, barbarism, and civilization could be observed in the present array of cultures, so Darwin was convinced that in matters of morality and intellect, differences "between the highest men of the highest races and the lowest savages are connected by the finest gradations," and that such gradualism in a static arrangement suggested the possibility that the highest forms had developed out of and through the other forms in the series.[25] It is difficult to tell when Darwin is talking about grades of social or cultural development and when the reference is strictly to the organic series, for he saw the former as an expression of the latter. Yet he appeared more willing to accept the continuity of the coexistent cultural series—the moral and mental life represented by the fine gradations of savagery and civilization. Breaks in the coexistent organic series (as known to us) he could not deny,[26] but he explained these as results of forms having become extinct. In both cases, however, the conversion of the coexistent series into a consecutive series was acceptable to Darwin, and in this he found himself in accord with a basic and longstanding tenet of cultural evolutionism.

Biologists must judge the merit of conceptually arranging observed differences among kinds of organisms for the purpose of representing a course of change through which organisms at one end of the gradation have come to be as they are, but the comparative method of depicting progress has not worked in the reconstruction of culture history. Darwin accepted the procedure as it had been applied by anthropologists and other humanists in the study of human culture, and he accepted their results. He also used the procedure in shaping his general view of the development of species—but now with the addition of an altogether distinct concept: natural selection.

The question that next arises is why students of society and culture did not seize on that powerful concept and turn it to their own purposes.

It has been argued that for nineteenth-century thinkers, the most disturbing elements in Darwin's theory of descent were its thoroughgoing materialism and its denial of purpose in an orderly process of change.[27] There is considerable merit in this. To social theorists of the time, for whom change was immanent in the thing changing, there was a note of futility in the suggestion that unsystematic alterations of environment acting on chance variations in the objects of change had resulted in a present unique and unpredictable array of differences. And the messiness of the idea was exacerbated by the corollary that analysis of that past process, and of the present hierarchy of differences, could yield no hint of what any future condition might be. Social evolutionists were searching for something much more satisfying than that, and it is understandable that even on this quite abstract level the Darwinian hypothesis had little to offer.

But Darwin's materialism in itself—his insistence on thought as a function of the brain, his denial of anything like a soul, his placement of man in the material world of other animals—should not be exaggerated as a barrier separating him from humanists of his day. Historians, philosophers, and social theorists had long been struggling with the materialism-idealism problem in the broadest sense and, whichever side they favored, they were not naïve on the issue. Darwin seems to have been particularly sensitive to the position of the Church regarding this matter, but that was not the stance of most of the hard-headed students of human culture and comparative institutions. Darwin and Huxley were more concerned about the opinions of Bishop Wilberforce than were Edward Burnett Tylor or Karl Marx.[28]

A more fruitful explanation of the limits of Darwinian influence on humanistic studies lies in the observation that Darwin did not work with any clear conception of human society and culture. In fact, he appeared to deny their existence, or at least their independence.

Darwin's failure to appreciate social and cultural influences was strikingly illustrated in his comparison of men and women. We should expect, he observed, by analogy, that men and women would differ: the bull differs from the cow, the boar from the sow, the stallion from the mare, and males of the larger apes from females. "Man," he asserted (without presenting evidence), "is more courageous, pugnacious and energetic than woman, and has a more inventive genius." While women excel in tenderness, unselfishness, intuition, and powers of rapid perception and imitation, we should, Darwin continued, bear in mind that at least some of these qualities are characteristic of "lower races" and, therefore, of a past and lower state of civilization. In anything requiring "deep thought, reason, or imagination, or merely the use of the senses and hands," however, men are preeminent. Thus,

If two lists were made of the most eminent men and women in poetry, painting, sculpture, music (inclusive both of composition and performance), history, science, and philosophy, with a half-a-dozen names under each subject, the two lists would not bear comparison.

It followed, for Darwin, that "the average of mental power in man must be above that of woman." [29]

It apparently did not occur to Darwin that the activities of women could have been shaped significantly by anything other than their biological attributes. That social rules or cultural expectations could have had anything substantial to do with who did what, and received what rewards or penalties, was evidently not a consideration.

This is clear, at one level, in Darwin's approach to the question of the source of human morality, values, and conscience. In his initial dealing with the problem, the source is either biological or supernatural; those are the only alternatives he seriously considers. These aspects of human cultures had their origin, Darwin would appear to argue, either in "the deeply planted social instinct," itself a product of organic development, or in "a special God-implanted conscience."[30] He measured the reasonableness and explanatory effectiveness of his biological account only against an account drawn from religion. He could not understand John Stuart Mill saying that morality is "natural" but that it is not "innate."[31] If it is not innate, then, Darwin seemed to imply, it has to be supernatural.

To scholars engaged in tracing the complicated processes by which individuals and peoples come by the particular value systems they have, such an orientation was irrelevant, at best. That persons went through a socialization process as a way to becoming human was not unknown in the middle of the nineteenth century, and it is difficult to see how Darwin could have been so little affected by the idea. That the individual products of this process *differ* within societies as well as between societies was evident. Humanists saw cultural value systems as results of complex historical processes, and while there was little agreement on the precise character of those processes, the fact that the products *differed* from place to place challenged the explanation that they were expressions of a common human instinct. If there was, indeed, a biological foundation to human values and morality, that had little to do with the particular problems in this area with which humanists were struggling. Given an effective and common human nature, the question of how it had expressed itself in such a variety of cultural forms remained uppermost.

At this other level, then, Darwin could offer little guidance to anthropologists and sociologists: he could not help them with their central problem of social and cultural differences, which was, for them, the problem of change.

He was aware of differences through time, as was any believer in the idea of progress, but he sought to explain differences in terms of biological change in individuals. The society with the largest number of men endowed with superior mental and moral powers, he argued, advances by virtue of that fact. Such powers are present in a certain amount because natural selection has favored them. Differences among societies, in degree of civilization achieved, are consequences of the varied operation of natural selection on human populations. It should be remembered, in this connection, that while Darwin regarded the *external* differences among human races as of no particular significance or use, and as products of sexual and not natural selection, he emphasized that this was not at all the case with "intellectual and moral or social faculties," which are, in his opinion, the very sources of civilization.[32]

This approach to the problem of cultural change and differences presented difficulties. For one thing, of course, it skipped over the question of which moral and mental powers are superior. Darwin was not troubled by doubts about the superiority of European intellect and virtue, and that provided him with a standard.[33] Such ethnocentrism in Darwin is understandable, for it was common as well among his colleagues in humanistic studies. It was by no means universal, however. It must be noticed, therefore, that here again Darwin did not provide an outlook that could have altered this aspect of humanistic study and led it to new perspectives.

A more serious difficulty lies in the fact that in discussing change and differences Darwin again ignored the existence of the social or cultural as such. A society, he inferred, is simply the product of the units composing it. The qualities of the units result in the quality of the society. Given populations composed of equal numbers of similarly endowed men, it follows that similar societies will result. This is to deny that historical experience has any other source or substance than in the individual biological qualities of men, and that historical processes have no effects in themselves. It is apparently irrelevant whether two such populations exist in Baghdad or Boston; in the fourth century B.C. or the twentieth A.D.; in a pastoral or a feudal agrarian economy; at a time when war and famine ravaged the land or peace and plenty blessed it; in a situation of intellectual darkness or in an efflorescence of learning.

It would be gratuitous to suppose that Charles Darwin could agree to such absurdity. But his argument leads to it by default. His emphasis is on an explanation of cultural similarities by the action of similar human natures. Tylor and Lubbock led him to believe that a fundamental likeness in tasks, dispositions, and habits prevails throughout the human species, and this testifies to like "inventive or mental powers" among different races. He thought it "extremely improbable" that similarities in bodily ornamentations, dancing, masquerading, and picture drawing are explicable in terms of tradition from a

53

common source or in terms of borrowing, and saw them rather as products of like minds. Cultural similarities could, therefore, be regarded as expressions of innate or instinctive human qualities. Darwin was aware, of course, that some cultural items are conventional and are acquired by individuals during their lifetimes; but he was not interested in such, for they offer no clue to innate sources of culture. In this respect he could be of no help to humanists who, like Tylor, were struggling to distinguish psychic unity, intercultural borrowing, and common cultural source as explanations of particular cultural similarities. Darwin was willing to accept a gross distinction: if it is widespread among "distinct races of man," it is innate or instinctive.[34]

What, then, about the problem of cultural differences? Darwin tended to approach the question at two levels. Concerning languages or minor particulars of culture content he is not specific, but the implication seems to be that such matters are either inexplicable or to be accounted for by chance. The difference between savagery and civilization, however, could hardly be disposed of in this manner. It was important to Darwin to keep the distinction between civilized and uncivilized peoples clear. He was no cultural relativist. Inasmuch as he leaned strongly toward the monogenist position in depicting the beginnings and history of the human species, the question could not be answered merely by postulating different races of varying potentials for civilization.

Darwin argued, we have noted, that the degree of advancement achieved by a society stands in direct relation to the number of highly endowed men in its population. That depends on the action of natural selection in the population, for there is a strong selection for those qualities in men that (1) serve them as individuals in the struggle for existence and reproduction and, at the same time, (2) result in their acting in such a way (energetically, courageously, loyally, intelligently, generously) as to advance their society in the civilizational scale.[35] It is, Darwin believed, by virtue of the differential presence of such qualities in populations that one nation comes to prevail over another and thus achieves a higher place in history.

A tribe including many members who, from possessing in a high degree the spirit of patriotism, fidelity, obedience, courage, and sympathy, were always ready to aid one another, and to sacrifice themselves for the common good, would be victorious over most other tribes; and this would be natural selection.[36]

If this process is to be referred to as *natural selection* of *tribal* attributes, then the reference can only be to attributes carried in the organic materials of inheritance (genes) for that is the only locus in which natural selection, as described by Darwin, operates. There can be no reference to tribal characteristics that are accountable to the tribe's geographical access to resources and protection or to its historical experiences. If we call the results of general competition and conflict among peoples natural selection, we are only drawing an analogy between a precisely organic process of differential reproduction in populations and that great complication of events that constitutes the histories of conflict between peoples.

That Darwin was indulging in metaphor at this point in his argument becomes apparent upon the failure of the metaphor to explain anything. For Darwin is, finally, left without an answer to the specific historical question of why Europeans are civilized and Hottentots are not (i.e., why concrete cultural differences exist). "It is . . . very difficult," he wrote, "to form any judgment why one particular tribe and not another has been successful and has risen in the scale of civilization." "Progress," he said, depends on many conditions, "far too complex to be followed out." It is "unreasonable," he thought, to ask why something happened in one country rather than in another. The problem of what initiates the movement of savages toward civilization is "at present much too difficult to be solved."[37]

It is very difficult to say why one civilized nation rises, becomes more powerful, and spreads more widely, than another; or why the same nation progresses more quickly at one time than at another. We can only say that it depends on an increase in the actual number of the population on the number of the men endowed with high intellectual and moral faculties, as well as on their standard of excellence.[38]

Once more, that was not a shining light to lead humanists in their struggle with the central question of cultural differences and the processes of change that could account for them. It should not be hard to understand why they did not flock to Darwinian leadership.

The concept of natural selection was not useful in accounting for cultural differences because it referred only to organic processes and because it was not a theory of history. Darwin never succeeded in linking naturally selected biological traits to actual sociocultural phenomena. Attempts to explain differences or "degrees" of civilization in terms of physical and psychological racial differences had been undergoing a revival in the years immediately preceding and accompanying Darwin's work. Such explanations, quite apart from their political implications, had not worked precisely because they omitted the social and cultural dimensions of the problem. It was a matter of deep concern to growing numbers of humanistic scholars that inquiry not be led down that blind path again. Darwin's suggestion, in 1871, that civilization was just a matter of good biology, was not helpful.

Humanists like Theodor Waitz, John Stuart Mill, and Henry Sumner Maine (all cited by Darwin, but in other contexts) realized the futility of biological accounts of cultural differences and were looking, at this time, for historical explanations of the rise of civilizations. That was a complex task, and it was apparently one with which Darwin had little sympathy. Unlike Darwin, men like Waitz regarded the question of why one people had risen higher in the scale of civilization than another as central to their inquiries. Other scholars engaged simply in the construction of ideal cultural series might continue with a "Darwinian methodology," but they clearly did not need to learn that from Darwin.

If Darwin's failure to account for social and cultural differences was assured by his failure to consider human, historical, social, and cultural events as relevant, it is instructive to notice that he himself was, to a degree, aware of that. His discussion of the origin and development of morality and virtue is complicated by an acceptance of the inheritance of effects produced by long habit, instruction, example, or use—the inheritance, in time, of acquired characters. Organic inheritance and transmission thus become indistinguishable in their effects from tradition, socialization, or enculturation.

For example, Darwin observes that humane treatment of lower animals, though based ultimately on a quite general sympathetic instinct, spreads by "instruction and example to the young" and is eventually encouraged by "public opinion." Here, more clearly than in the case of organic structural features, Darwin is in need of something other than chance variation and natural selection to account for change.

Even the partial transmission of virtuous tendencies would be an immense assistance to the primary impulse derived directly and indirectly from the social instincts. Admitting for a moment that virtuous tendencies are inherited, it appears probable, at least in such cases as chastity, temperance, humanity to animals, etc., that they become first impressed on the mental organization through habit, instruction and example, continued during several generations in the same family, and in a quite subordinate degree, or not at all, by the individuals possessing such virtues having succeeded best in the struggle for life.[39]

The "primary impulse" tends more and more to become a biological given for Darwin as he struggles with the history of human morality. Natural selection is replaced by learning as men come to use their intellectual powers for discerning remote consequences of acts, rejecting baneful customs and beliefs, and profiting from habit, instruction, and example. Thus, Western Europeans owe little or none of their high achievement to direct inheritance from the classical Greeks, "though they owe much to the written works of that wonderful people." The struggle for existence and natural selection, especially in civilized societies, must, therefore, assume a position subordinate to other agencies in producing "the highest part of man's nature." The "fundamental social instincts" originally produced by natural selection seem to lose their effectiveness for Darwin in accounting for what goes on in civilized societies.[40]

The biological factor thus fades in the course of human

history and one is apparently left by Darwin with the task of explaining in cultural terms concrete cultural changes and differences. Humanists who read Darwin could only agree. Furthermore, Darwin's insistence on an *ultimate* organic basis for human history, a basis that should be viewed in continuity with other animal forms, could hardly have disturbed scholars exposed to a European intellectual tradition in which that broad conception of man and his place in nature was commonplace.

The failure of social scientists in the second half of the nineteenth century, and since, to shape their inquiries in a Darwinian mold is explicable, then, by the facts that (1) he offered an already familiar theory of change and method for reconstructing processes of change; (2) he failed to shed light, by his concept of natural selection, on the central problem of cultural differences; and (3) he effectively denied a subject matter for social and cultural sciences, except for a belated and ad hoc recognition of it that contained no new solutions or avenues to solutions of problems long recognized.

It is unreasonable to expect more from Darwin. To the extent that he depended on traditionally oriented anthropologists and sociologists of his day, he was, of course, revealing nothing new. He made no study of human societies and cultures outside the quite limited inquiries connected with *The Expression of the Emotions in Man and Animals.* His demonstration of man's relatedness to other animals and his case for biological foundations of human intellectual, moral, and social life turned out, partly on his own testimony, to be irrelevant to explications of cultural change and cultural differences.

Perhaps humanists should simply continue to recognize that they and Darwinists are asking different, though related, questions, and to let the matter rest. But that is a difficult posture to maintain while being accused of blindness for failing to see the obvious path for a science of man that Charles Darwin showed us. So, humanists may be excused for noticing not only that Darwin did no such thing, but also that he associated his name and authority with some misleading notions of his and our own time.

CHAPTER 3

SOCIOBIOLOGY AND THE HUMAN SCIENCES

In 1962, Theodosius Dobzhansky noted that the causes of the origin, progress, and decline of civilizations remain undiscovered and that, while the possibility of genetic factors being involved in these processes should not be dismissed out of hand, clearly they are not the principal factors. He had noted earlier that the weighing of genotypic and environmental variables in explanation of important human differences, including cultural differences, is a subject on which we know little or nothing. While he would not agree that genetic variability affecting the capacity to learn has "suddenly evaporated" in human populations, he was inclined to let matters stand with the observation that human evolution has interrelated and interdependent biological and cultural components, and with the expressed hope for mutual understanding between biologists and anthropologists on the problem.[1]

Recently, some biologists have taken a much bolder stand on these issues and have developed a position that commands attention. Sociobiologists propose to carry the implications of Darwinian theory and the substance of the modern theory of organic evolution to the frontier of current biological concern with human nature and culture.

If the reaction of humanists to this venture has not been enthusiastic, it must be recalled that they have not simply overlooked the biological basis of their subject. They did not, as the preceding chapters have demonstrated, absentmindedly ignore the obvious relevance of Darwinism to their concerns. The concepts of culture and of society were formulated in direct response to observed failures of repeated efforts by both humanists and biologists to explicate human activities in organic terms.[2] Serious scholarly reservation has proceeded from the plain observation that biological analysis of human social life has not thus far explained anything, and has had the effect of stopping the search for explanation.

If, then, the new biology of man is to command serious attention within the human sciences today, it must identify more surely than earlier studies the contents of human nature and demonstrate more convincingly a causal relationship between those contents and the actual activities of people. If genetic tendencies in people have brought about significant features of the social and cultural results observable to us, then it is clearly of great importance that anybody trying to account for those results inquire into the existence and operation of such tendencies.

The first task of sociobiology, then, is to establish, as fact, the influence of genes on the production of sociocultural phenomena. It is apparently with this obligation in mind that Edward O. Wilson has said that the objective must be to *measure* the amount of influence genes exercise in producing behavioral qualities that underlie culture.[3] Humanists who would look to biologists for guidance must be vitally interested in this crucial operation.

If one attended only to the existing quantitative evidence of stipulated genes producing designated human social and cultural actions, the task of measuring the amount of the influence might be abruptly foreclosed. One eminent geneticist and prominent critic of sociobiology has said that at this time there is "not a vestige of evidence" that any of the human traits sociobiologists talk about have any genetic basis.[4] Professor Wilson himself has acknowledged candidly that the ability of biologists to identify specifically any genes that influence human behavior will come only in the future.[5]

To stop with this, however, would not only do injustice to the persuasiveness of the sociobiological argument in its more general aspects, but it would leave unexplained, and, therefore, unaltered, the vulnerability of conventional social theory to a thesis that is supported by so fragile a foundation of data. It is necessary, then, to take a more comprehensive look at what is involved in biology's latest effort to throw light on the history of man.[6]

Schematically, sociobiology begins with the observation that man is only one among many social species and human social behavior is only one sort among a great array. It is argued, therefore, that students of society should take the whole range of social creatures as their field and thereby reap the usual benefits of comparison—a deeper understanding of what is characteristic of any given species and the formation of more comprehensive and broadly supported generalizations. In particular, however, it is suggested that success experienced by biologists in explaining social behavior in nonhuman animals can be emulated by social scientists. Sociobiologists are not generally inclined to see this as a reciprocal affair, quite obviously on the ground that the social sciences and humanities at this time have nothing fundamental to contribute because they are dealing with surface phenomena by virtue of their failure to seek a materialist, biological foundation of human behavior. Once informed by biological insights, it is granted, the social sciences can be expected to outstrip biology in richness of content, but as matters stand they are regarded as having isolated no proper subject matter.[7]

In studying "the social" across species, sociobiologists propose identification of elements in behavior that are to be regarded as organic units in the same sense as spleens or lungs or apposable thumbs. The repertory of human behaviors is not detailed at any length, although an intention to fill out the human biogram is announced. Sociobiologists display a special concern, however, with aggression, altruism, and sex as elemental categories of behavior. To this common trinity, Wilson adds a "predisposition to religious belief" as the "most complex and powerful force in the human mind and in all probability an ineradicable part of human nature."[8] It is altruistic behavior, however, that is taken as the basic ingredient of any society, and it is in an explanation of such behavior that sociobiology claims a major accomplishment. All of these features or elements of human nature are subsumed under a universal propensity in individuals to enhance their inclusive genetic fitness—i.e., to act in such a way as to improve one's reproductive advantage in the broadest sense.

If behaviors are organic units, the argument continues, their existence is to be explained in the same way that other organic traits are explained—by evolution through natural selection. This is the heart of the sociobiological thesis and the feature that distinguishes it from the pre-Darwinian study of human nature. It is pointed out that we readily accept behaviors in other animals as genetically based and as products of natural selection. Significant behaviors in humans must be explained in the same way, if there is such a thing as human nature, and if there are genetic components of human nature. To argue otherwise, Wilson points out, would involve identifying a new form of genetic change in populations and subverting fundamental evolutionary theory. A behavior is to be understood, then, as prevailing in a species because it is adaptive, that is, because it contributes to the genetic fitness of persons—to increased personal survival, to increased personal reproduction, and to increased survival and reproduction of kin who share the same genes.[9]

A basic purpose of this effort by sociobiologists to identify and account for the elements of human nature is the creation of a scientific ethic for mankind. Knowledge of what we ought to do, it is claimed, must be derived from a knowledge of what we are. The search for self-knowledge must proceed free of all illusions and false pride. We must be ready to acknowledge that a very important part of the human behavioral repertory makes sense only in light of the genetic advantage it confers on individuals. A materialist base for a realistic ethic is to be sought, therefore, in a biological analysis of human nature. Barring a distant and problematic ability to engineer a different genetic make-up for man, we are said to be in the presence of a relatively stable and stubborn set of characteristics that must be accepted as the foundation of a workable ethical system.[10]

An additional feature of sociobiological analysis that is of special interest to social scientists is the contention that societies, including the human kinds, are statistical results of the behavior of their individual components. There is, according to this view, no superorganic such as Kroeber sought to distinguish. There is no cultural dynamic as such. There are no societies as such—only populations. Sociobiologists realize that this denies to anthropology and sociology their traditional subject matter, and they recognize that this circumstance is responsible for part of the resistance to the new synthesis.[11]

In reacting to these specific features of sociobiology and trying to assess the extent to which they promise more than traditional human-nature study, social scientists might note at the outset that so far as the concrete contents of human nature are concerned, the new biology accepts a conventional picture. The tendencies, drives, predispositions, or instincts identified as having a genetic basis have generally been regarded for a long time as lying deep within man. (See chapter 1.) It would appear that there has been substantial agreement among Western observers on the constituent elements of human nature, although the relative strengths or effects of the elements have been disputed. The contexts of both old and new discussions of the matter strongly suggest that the list has usually been compiled from casual observation, anecdote, and an abiding consensus. There were some rather sophisticated eighteenth-century analyses of human nature, but their basis was always somewhat unsystematic observation of how people had typically acted in typical circumstances. Sociobiologists would appear to proceed in the same way. For them, widespread incidence of a behavior suggests a controlling genetic base in human nature; variations in culture are taken to "provide clues to underlying genetic differences."[12] What is given, to sociobiologists and social scientists alike, is people acting, and the acts are classified as aggressive, cooperative, altruistic, and so on. The categories of action are largely agreed upon.

In this connection, one source of needless argument is the belief of some sociobiologists that their representation of prevailing patterns of human behavior is more realistic than that offered by humanists and social scientists.[13] Certainly it is possible to find in the humanistic literature idealized representations of moral sentiments in man, but it is as easy to find (see chapter 1) exactly the picture of human nature that sociobiology urges us to accept.[14] Jeremy Bentham might properly complain that sociobiologists have recreated precisely his views on the immediate springs of human action, and have not done as tidy a job of it.

The serious point for consideration here is, however, the sociobiological thesis that the effective attributes of human nature, whether these move people to aggression or dominance or altruism or religion or territorialism or whatever, all have as their function the promotion of behavior that augments reproductive advantage. This is a functional organization and interpretation of human nature traits by the use of Darwinian evolutionary theory. Bentham could arrange all human behavioral characteristics under a general pattern of pleasure seeking and pain avoidance, but he had no convincing explanation of why or to what end a person sought pleasure and avoided pain, or how he had come to act that way. He observed only that one had to start somewhere in an inquiry about man and he was going to begin with the obvious fact that people do act from utilitarian considerations (see chapter 4). This is not a simple matter of infinite regression. If the sociobiologist is asked why people behave so as to improve their genetic fitness, he can argue that the very evolutionary process that shaped people could have shaped their behavior only in that way. As Barash has pointed out, it is one thing to identify elements in human nature, or to specify innate structures in the manner of Piaget or Chomsky, but quite another to explain why such elements or structures exist and why we might expect to find others like them.[15]

This means that sociobiology claims that its characterization of human nature and its stipulation of the effects of human nature are given authenticity by a demonstration of how traits of human nature have a genetic base and are, therefore, products of natural selection. In this way, it is said, behaviors that are inexplicable in terms of rational human choices can be accounted for by the biological fitness they bestow on individuals so behaving. Biological fitness consists immediately in survival and reproduction, but essentially, from the sociobiological point of view, the sign and measure of fitness is the amount of one's genes, relative to the different genes of others, that appear in succeeding generations. The process of survival of the fittest humans can therefore be represented as the success of certain gene complexes in equipping human carriers so that they behave in such a way as to become successful vehicles for the replication of those same gene complexes.[16]

The claim is, then, that human social behavior is, in some significant measure, controlled by, restrained by, monitored or mediated by heritable units we call genes. What these units are and what their conglomerate effects are at any given time and place are always results, so far as we know, of natural selection. These propositions take on definiteness and meaning with an accompanying denial that human social behavior is entirely, or most significantly, a product of the social experiences of people.

If this is to be accepted as an accurate picture of what is going on in human populations, it might seem reasonable to ask for evidence that specified adaptive behaviors have actually resulted, in successive generations, in a relatively larger number of genes or gene complexes that are demonstrably responsible for those behaviors. The science of genetics is at present apparently unable to produce such data, however, and evidence of a different and indirect nature is offered in the form of examples of widespread types of human behavior that can, according to the claim, be best explained by their contribution to genetic fitness.

Thus incest taboos are accounted for by suggesting that, since incest results in relative genetic unfitness, the number of persons with a genetic predisposition for incest avoidance will tend to increase in any given population. Again, female infanticide in India and China might be understood, it is said, as part of a genetically determined reproductive strategy adaptive in conditions where males of a given class have a greater chance of passing on parental genes. Inheritance in the male line, it is argued, could derive from the fact that it is more efficient in maximizing ancestral fitness than is transmission of wealth along the female line. Aggressive human behavior is represented as genetically based because it is widespread, its forms are species-specific, and it has, at least in the past, conferred a biological advantage. Altruistic behavior is explained by the principle of inclusive genetic fitness: acts that decrease an individual's chance for survival can, at the same time, so increase the chances for survival of others like him that there is a net increase in the genes for altruistic behavior in the population. Religious behavior is explicable, according to Wilson, by the fact that it favors the survival and reproduction of practitioners by giving them an identity, a sense of commitment or purpose in life, and a definition of place or mission in history.[17]

Because sociobiologists see all genetically mediated behavior as being ultimately explicable by reference to the reproductive advantage the behavior confers, they often seek illustrations of genetic control in activities bearing directly on mating and child-rearing. Natural selection is supposed to favor a disposition to choose mates who will provide the best chance of reproductive success. Those human features that prove attractive to a prospective mate should correlate, therefore, with features that support reproductive potential. This is said to be the case: good physique, regular features, and smooth complexion, for example, fit both requirements. If it appears that some physical features—broad hips in women, which facilitate childbirth—no longer demonstrate this correlation, the matter is explained by the fact that modern medicine has made that feature unnecessary. In like manner, it is argued that since older men are more likely to command resources needed by a reproducing female, natural selection should result in a propensity in women to favor maturity in men; and, indeed, men are older than their mates in most societies.

The double standard in promiscuity among males and females is understandable biologically, it is claimed, because the genetic fitness of men is more seriously threatened by extramural sexual activities of their mates than the fitness of women is by male dalliance. By similar reasoning, frequency of divorce should correlate with degrees of decreased reproductive potential, i.e., persons should be genetically disposed to leave mates when there are signs of reproductive weakness. The frequent annulment of unconsummated marriages is said to testify to the existence of such a tendency. The greater reluctance of couples to divorce when they have children is, once more, said to be in keeping with a genetic drive to safeguard an investment in reproductive potential. Again, if two women, ages nineteen and thirty-eight, are in a position where they must choose to save themselves or their babies from death, sociobiological theory predicts that the older woman would be more inclined than the younger to save her baby, on the ground that there has been natural selection for greater investment in current offspring among parents with less reproductive potential.[18]

Data bearing on genetic determination of human behavior are also drawn from pathology and from identical twin studies. It is claimed that changes in the chemical composition of genes or in arrangements of chromosomes have been correlated with neurological disorders and diminished intelligence. Testing of identical and fraternal twins is said to reveal that for a given trait the former resemble each other on the average more than the latter do, and, given appropriate controls for environmental influences, this is taken to provide a measure of the genetic control over traits that could be regarded as affecting social behavior.[19] Materials of this sort are of great interest and will no doubt continue to command attention. They are not heavily relied on by sociobiologists, however, because the data are still quite meager and their relevance to basic categories of social behavior is not always clear.

As regards this kind of indirect evidence of naturally selected genetic controls on human social behavior, and the forms of the argument using such evidence, the following difficulties are indicated.

First, the response of sociobiologists to a call for evidence supporting their general theorems has been limited seriously by their belief that non-European tribal societies, or peoples known only through sparse archaeological evidence, will reveal most clearly the true nature of man and the sources of cultural basics in that nature. This means that they are usually examining situations in which demographic data for extended periods are practically nonexistent. For example, it has been argued that the Mundurucú headhunters of Brazil came to engage in aggressive behavior because it actually improved their access to protein (peccaries) and so enhanced their reproductive fitness, even though they have been entirely unaware of this function of their warfare.[20] In instances of this kind the logic of natural selection stands alone, for there is no available evidence that the benefits of perilous warfare outweighed the losses, or even that there was a real relationship between human headhunting and peccary hunting. The argument is persuasive only when anecdotal evidence is checked against a conceptual model. It is asking a great deal, of course, that in such a situation demographic data be produced that would demonstrate selection for a genetically mediated capacity for effective aggressive behavior. But the conclusions drawn from such studies are not insignificant.

Second, a pervasive difficulty attending verification of a genetic base for an adaptive behavior is that adaptiveness in itself cannot be taken as a sure sign of natural selection at work. As Wilson has pointed out, people obviously *learn* ways of acting that increase their biological fitness.[21] All that might be needed from organic evolution, then, is a capacity for learning, or, as it is sometimes put, a capacity for culture, in order to account for any given behavioral adaptation. The problem posed here is, apparently, another variation of the old nature-nurture dilemma—a dilemma that continues to plague us despite repeated assertion that it is not a real problem. Wilson's characterization of adaptation through learning as "cultural mimicry" of "more structured forms of biological adaptation" would seem to beg the question. His argument that the genes hold culture on a leash implies that natural selection would remove any behavior that worked to significant reproductive disadvantage, but natural selection works only on genetically based characteristics. If a behavior is "purely cultural," to use Wilson's expression, the question of how natural selection can affect it is bothersome unless we accept some sort of Lamarckian framework. The close fit of human social behavior to the requirement that it enhance biological fitness could be perfect even if all behavior were purely cultural; and there is no a priori reason to suppose, as

Wilson evidently does, that the strength or automatic nature of genetically constrained behavior is any greater than the strength or automatic nature of cultural behavior. Such characteristics would not appear, then, appropriate for distinguishing the two. We are back to the problem of measuring the amount of genetic influence in any given behavior.

Third, the procedures followed by biologists in demonstrating the underlying genetic factors in clear cases of organic traits are not apparent in their efforts to explain human social actions genetically. Wilson, for example, reminds us that, since no biological trait is entirely the product of genes, when we speak of genetic determination we refer to determination of some *difference* of a given trait in two or more compared instances of its appearance. Thus, genes do not produce blue eyes, but the difference between blue and brown eyes is explicable in terms of genes. This is done by gathering information on the eye color of parents and other relatives, comparing these data with a model of Mendelian heredity, and feeding in knowledge about cell multiplication and sexual reproduction. In the same way, Wilson argues, the existence and amount of genetic influence in the production of a human social behavior can be revealed by, first, a comparison with that social behavior in other animals, and, second, comparison of different forms of a social behavior within and among human populations.

In the comparison of humans and other primates, Wilson claims that both the similarities and differences in their behaviors testify to the behaviors being genetically based. The similarities in behavior between humans and chimpanzees are said to be so marked that, taken together with anatomical and biochemical evidence, they must "at least in part" be based on identical genes. Wilson then argues that the differences between human and other primate social behavior are so distinct that they must be based on a unique set of human genes. This reasoning is hard to follow unless we start from a premise that there is a genetic basis for behaviors. Then it might follow that the basis should be most clearly marked where the behaviors were most strikingly similar or most strikingly different. But the premise here is the point in question. Taking only the evidence of similarities and differences in human and chimpanzee behavior one could argue as well that they are the result of lunar influence.

In the comparison of individual differences within populations and differences between populations, the effort to identify and isolate the hereditary element is more successful, but the traits analyzed are not clearly diagnostic of humanity. This latter comparison is admittedly beset by great difficulties, especially since it involves the sociobiologist in the old and bitter question of racial differences and racial explanations of cultural differences,[22] a problem we shall have occasion to return to.

The criticism here, however, is that when sociobiologists move from a relatively simple or clear-cut level of genetic analysis of a specific trait to the level of demonstrating a genetic basis for essential humanness, the analytical rigor of the former procedure gives way to a hint or an analogy or what comes very close to a mere assertion that the uniformity of nature guarantees that what is genetically controlled at level A is genetically controlled at level B.[23] To the layman, there is slight connection between the procedure by which the geneticist demonstrates the determination of blueness as a difference in eyes and, for example, monotheism as a difference in religions. It seems reasonable to ask for a clear procedural example in the latter category that would parallel the use of the Mendelian model of heredity in accounting for eye color, especially in light of the fact that sociobiologists are equivocal about their interpretation of human social or cultural differences.

Similar reservations are in order regarding the manner in which connections between biological and cultural phenomena are made in terms of genetic *capacities*. To say, for example, that humans have genes "enabling" them to be aggressive could be a problematic statement if it were a question of whether it is genes or some other organic disposition that is responsible. But surely there can be no disputing the fact that humans are able to be aggressive, and there is little guidance in that observation when we are already aware from historical evidence of warfare and other forms of violence in human experience.[24] To the extent that sociobiological theory can direct attention to historical phenomena hitherto unnoticed, it must be valuable. And when it can suggest lines of explanation that go beyond a designation of capacities for general behavior patterns underlying such phenomena, social theorists must be expected to respond. But to observe merely that there has been natural selection for capacities to carry on a social or cultural activity is of limited significance as long as the variations on which selection works occur in a genetic base that is so general as to serve a great variety of such activities. Then the range of possible cultural results is not explicable by natural selection.

Fourth, and in like vein, if what is "truly new" about sociobiology is a demonstration of how "social groups adapt to the environment by evolution,"[25] that should be done for some actual human social groups, with careful distinction between and, one would hope, measurements of, adaptations by natural selection and adaptations by learning. It would be of great interest to students of human societies and cultures to look at even a projected extension of such analysis to the problem of cultural differences. If what we are given in any array of human societies and cultures are basically adaptations in a Darwinian sense, the problem of differences is a problem of adaptive requirements and adaptive alternatives. Various environments presumably impose various problems of existence on organisms, and permit a variety of solutions. Can we, then, account for the differences between a hunter-gatherer society and an industrial society in terms of adaptation to environment? If, as Wilson has remarked, civilization is linked to humans only by accident, must we also say that it is only by accident that it has appeared among some populations of humans and not others, or can we go beyond Darwin on that matter?

Fifth, a line of sociobiological argument that is likely to be questioned by social scientists is the contention that where the behavior of persons is not comprehended by the observer as rational, there is a likelihood that such behavior is genetically controlled. For example, Wilson argues that female hypergamy and infanticide "do not recommend themselves" as rational conduct, and the inference is that if they are not to be explained as acts of reason, then they are to be explained as proceeding from an inherited predisposition to maximize offspring.[26] The possibility that what looks like nonrational behavior to the observer might be quite rational to the actor has long posed a serious problem for social scientists seeking an understanding of human activities through inquiry into the intentions of the persons involved. A suggestion that behavior that does not "recommend itself" as rational to the sociobiologist must therefore be a product of genetic traits will probably be questioned by students of human affairs who have succeeded only recently and after long struggle in accepting a primary obligation to understand puzzling social phenomena in their own terms. There has long been an unfortunate tendency to simplify the complex in human activities, to capture the unfamiliar in familiar boxes. Sociobiologists must expect that social scientists are now likely to be extremely wary of any general solvent for problems posed by social and cultural behavior, at least until the evidence goes well beyond the level of speculation about the genetic basis of nonrational conduct.

Sixth, clarification of the sociobiological message to anthropologists and sociologists depends on a mutual understanding of what is spoken of as social or cultural evolution. The idea that an abstract human society or culture has passed through a process of gradual historical change, that the process has been a movement through stages that can be represented by different societies and cultures observable to us in the present or with the help of historical evidence, and that, in the broadest sense, some existing societies and cultures have changed more in the process than others—this idea, which is very much older than the Darwinian theory of organic evolution, is generally accepted by sociobiologists. There is no reluctance to accept a historical condition of one people (an existing hunter-gatherer tribe) as representative of the earlier historical condition of another people (an existing industrial society), and apparently with all the implications for the notion of unilinear culture change that such methodology carries.

One might expect in this situation that sociobiologists would be interested in depicting a human organic evolution of which human social evolution is an expression. Darwin did not go into the details, but it is clear that he saw higher, or civilized, human society as a product of an evolutionary process in which natural selection for higher intellectual and moral qualities had gone on in some populations to a greater extent than in others. He was, as we have noted, obscure in his recognition of social or cultural transmission in the process, but he was clear enough on the basic significance of natural selection in the production of people who made civilization possible, as distinguished from people who made it impossible. Sociobiologists appear to go no further along this path than the cautious position from which the capacity for culture is seen as a product of organic evolution. Cultural differences to them have no clear biological significance. What happens in one particular time or place in history that is different from what happens in another is not taken to be a product of genetic evolution. On the contrary, Wilson draws a distinction between genetic and cultural evolution that allows him to define the one by the absence of the other. Thus he is ready to see hunter-gatherer existence as an expression of hereditary qualities, but since there is no appreciable genetic difference between twentieth-century hunter-gatherers and people in advanced industrial nations, the cultural change involved in the appearance of civilization cannot be regarded, he argues, as a result of any significant genetic change. This leads him to the extraordinary statement that the human social and cultural changes that have occurred in the last ten thousand years "were created by cultural rather than genetic evolution."[27] When evolution is defined as "any gradual change" we are left with the proposition that cultural change is created by cultural change.[28] This is in keeping with an orientation from which all history not produced by genetic controls is regarded as accidental and therefore incomprehensible in ultimate terms.[29] Far from seeking a rapprochement between theories of genetic and cultural change, therefore, some sociobiologists seem to insist on a radical distinction between the two processes during the entire historical period of man.

For the prehistoric period—say five million years prior to changes in the hunter-gatherer culture—human social behavior is represented as a product, to an important extent, of genetic changes. Because evidence for social behavior in that period is so scarce, sociobiologists feel compelled to seek data on the genetic control of human social life in observations of modern, non-European, tribal peoples whose economies are presumed to be similar to those of prehistoric man. Use of such evidence is allowable, of course, only on the assumption that we know what prehistoric social life was like, and that was the knowledge being sought in the first place. The use of cultural differences for the reconstruction of history is no less problematic for twentieth-century sociobiologists than for the eighteenth- and nineteenth-century progress theorists.

Sociobiologists have come to this complicated stance on the question of cultural evolution by virtue of their conviction that, while natural selection can generally be expected to result in the adaptation of behavior to life conditions, in the instance of human social behavior that was true for five million years but has not been true for the last ten thousand years for people living in "advanced" societies. People in this later period carry genetic dispositions evolved in response to primitive life conditions, and many of those dispositions are said to be no longer serviceable in modern times. In fact, tendencies like aggression have become so threatening to genetic fitness that they jeopardize human existence itself. Konrad Lorenz presented this idea to the public in his *On Aggression*, and it has become a cornerstone of sociobiological theory.[30] The notion has important implications for social policy and social action and so has engendered controversy. What is of particular interest in the context of the present discussion, however, is the suggestion in all this that something has been going on in human history that not only has not been controlled by genes but has run directly counter to genetic advantage. Somehow adaptations have become counter-adaptive. How does sociobiological analysis make sense of that?

Wilson and Barash attempt to explain this predicament by a statement that cultural evolution moves *faster* than genetic evolution. Thus, changes in the genetic structure of a population are said to proceed by necessarily minute increments over many generations, while vast changes in a culture can come about in the space of a single human lifetime, and newness so acquired can spread and augment by communications and transmissions unknown in the realm of organic evolution. Cultural evolution is therefore characterized as Lamarckian, while biological evolution is Darwinian.

Now, if the speed of those actions in nature that we call organic evolution is to be compared with the speed of those actions within human societies that we call cultural evolution, some time and unit measure is required.[31] When the problem is stated in that way, it becomes evident that what is being observed here is not a cultural process moving faster than an organic process, but people who are judged to be acting in ways that threaten their genetic fitness. From a layman's point of view the observation might simply be—as it has been so often—that people do not seem to be acting in their own best interests.

The argument from genetic lag is forceful, given any measure of genetic influence on human social behavior. The possibility that attributes shaped by evolution under one set of conditions would no longer be serviceable in another is clear. The probability that natural selection, like all biological processes, will not work to perfection, and so will leave discrepancies between genotype and environment, seems in keeping with modern theory of organic evolution. Wilson takes this view when he observes that there is a "biological refractoriness" that does not allow genetic propensity to relatively weak culture to continue beyond a certain point, and thus "biological evolution will begin to pull cultural evolution back to itself." But what is provocative about sociobiology's presentation of such alleged facts is the question it raises about processes of human history. If, as Wilson says, biological evolution is *always* outrun by cultural change, and *quickly,* we are not faced with anything extraordinary when we find a lack of fit between existing genes for social behavior and a prevailing society. And if cultural change is fortuitous when it is anything other than a direct product of biological change, then ten thousand years of human history—all of human cultural history as we really know it—has to be comprehended largely as an error. It certainly cannot be seen as a continuous process of organic evolution, and cultural evolution is, from the sociobiological perspective, evidently mishmash.

Yet, if we assume that human nature has been relatively constant for the last ten thousand years, the cultural changes that have taken place during that time call for explanation in some way. An inviting way out of this paradox might appear to lie in recognizing that populations of humans react variously to the lag situation. In some, natural selection pulls back or acts more quickly on available variations to achieve readaptation; others lose the race and are replaced. Thus Wilson, in a context of biological and cultural evolution asserts: "Societies that decline because of a genetic propensity of its [sic] members to generate competitively weaker cultures will be replaced by those more appropriately endowed."[32]

His immediate disclaimer of any intent to explain the "relative performances" of modern societies by genetic differences is unlikely to persuade his critics that his position here is different from Darwin's conclusion that natural selection works to the elevation of some peoples and the extinction of others. Alternative explanations of "relative performances" are lacking in both Darwin and Wilson.

The aim here is to suggest that misunderstanding of sociobiologists' views on such questions might be prevented by clarification of what they mean by cultural evolution and a fuller specification of relationships between organic and cultural evolution. This could sharpen the dialogue with social scientists on substantive issues, and one might even hope that it would reduce the sometimes acrid quality of the sociobiology debate.

It seems clear, in any event, that the core elements of sociobiological theory that distinguish it from older human-nature studies are the arguments (1) that human nature consists, to some important extent, in a set of genetic components that control social behavior, and (2) that the components are products of natural selection.

The above brief review of evidence for these propositions reveals no hard data of a kind many geneticists call for in the ordinary course of their work. Instead, there has been an impressive presentation of human behaviors, customs, and institutions that seem to be explicable by a theory that says there would be a strong selection for biological traits in persons to act in these ways because it gives them reproductive advantage over others. That, rather than concrete evidence, is the main source of sociobiology's great appeal: the powerfully compelling logic of natural selection, a conceptual tool that earlier human-nature theorists did not have at their disposal.

The ingenuity displayed by Trivers, DeVore, Wilson, Barash, Ghiselin, Dawkins, and more recent sociobiologists in showing how a behavior is adaptive and how it could therefore have come to be selected for, is striking and persuasive. Allegedly puzzling kinds of human conduct suddenly become understandable in the light of relatively simple calculations of genetic advantage, and an exciting hope for a new avenue of social and cultural inquiry is kindled. There can be no question that these

84

clues and suggestions call for attention and possible development in all branches of human inquiry.

But the concept of natural selection can also be seen as a possible source of weakness in the study of human activities, even for those interested only in biological analysis. It can be pressed to explain too much. If it is taken as a statement about something going on in nature, it is particularly susceptible to the kind of abuse that stretches an idea to comprehend the universe. Where it is so difficult to distinguish between genetic and nongenetic results, especially in behavior, it is obviously of the greatest importance to support the genetic explanation with concrete evidence and to be mindful of the evidence for a nongenetic explanation. Instead, sociobiologists seem to proceed with a conviction that any human behavior of basic significance must be explicable by natural selection theory. With that premise, the aim is to find, not what actually occasioned the behavior, but how it *could* have been produced by natural selection. As Thelma Rowell has argued so cogently,[33] if explanation from natural selection is not taken as a hypothesis to be tested, the practice of finding adaptive import in practically anything can become a sort of parlor game. That is what often seems to be going on when sociobiologists hone their wits to find reproductive advantage in, for example, homosexual or spiteful behavior. By postulating enough hypothetical circumstances it becomes possible to explain anything as a result of natural selection. There is a tendency to forget that the reality necessary to the explanation has only been postulated.

From a more general standpoint, sociobiologists must try to understand why social scientists are not likely to rally just yet under the banner of the "new synthesis." Sociobiologists readily admit that most social behavior is nongenetic, that most culture history is not biological history. By their own judgment they are engaged, insofar as they are dealing with humans at least, in a speculative venture. The core of Professor Wilson's only work on man is quite properly described by him as a "speculative essay."[34] The evidence that bears on his thesis is slight and uncertain. David Barash states he does not know if sociobiology will shed light on human social behavior, but he thinks it "worth trying." What he writes about humans is, he says, "frankly speculative" and even "a bit outrageous." Barash seems aware of the dangers that lie in facile explanations by natural selection, and, noting that he is only *assuming* that what is true of other animals is true of humans, he invites us to play "Let's Pretend" and "see where it takes us."[35] Richard Dawkins writes ten fascinating chapters that lead up to a description of how genes guide human social behavior, and then in the eleventh retreats with an elementary sociological disquisition on processes of human socialization.[36] So, while much of sociobiology is fascinating, and no holds are to be barred in grappling with problems of social life, it is too much to expect that many social scientists would drop what they are doing and join in a venture still so unformed.

Darwin's theory of natural selection offered a better account than any other, in 1859, of how the different forms of life on earth have come to be. Darwin had to cope with theological explanations at one level and teleological biology at another, and he did so by offering better explanations and evidence, not by condemning religion and philosophy. It is of the utmost importance to communication between humanists and biologists today that the extension of Darwinism to the study of human affairs be seen as a different matter. To the extent that sociobiological theory is offered as a corrective to a supernaturally oriented teleology believed to characterize the social sciences, it is likely to be simply ignored by anthropologists and sociologists. The religious and philosophical propositions that appear to have troubled Darwin have not been taken seriously by most humanists since the seventeenth century and are not evident in the halls of social science today. Sociobiologists have an obligation to meet the social and cultural sciences on their own empirical grounds—the histories of peoples as they are known to us by the record. There is little point in tilting at theological windmills. Darwin's mistake in supposing that the only possible alternative explanations of human society are the biological and the supernatural is being repeated today by sociobiologists.[37]

Finally, the new ethic sociobiologists propose to create has engendered some uneasiness among the laity. However, the concern might be unfounded. The new scientific ethic is hardly a radical departure from the old. In content its central admonitions are to avoid harming others, to forgo tribalism and receive the whole human species as our kin, to be tolerant of others different from ourselves, and to recognize the right of all persons to life. These are not, of course, offered as new values; but whereas they are said to have once had only an intuitive or otherwise mysterious base, they are now recommended for their biological validity. The rightness of such rules is said to flow from our essential mammalian nature.

But now the age-old problem: Why are we not obeying

the rules dictated by our very nature for the sake of that nature? The answer sociobiologists supply here is the lag theory. We are said to be burdened with a phylogenetic heritage that makes it very difficult for us to behave in ways proper to our present situation. We carry within us qualities our fathers acquired in a distant past. Is everything carried over from the past bad? No, we inherit both good and bad. Then how shall we decide, as Wilson puts it, "which of the elements of human nature to cultivate and which to handle with care," especially when it would appear that our decisions must be made under the influence of our heritage? And the answer is that through an exercise of will, a conscious resolve, and the pursuit of self-knowledge we can break this circle and come to a realization of what is right and then teach that. Will such knowledge emancipate us from the hard biological bonds that hold us captive, and can we then enter upon a free existence here on earth? No, that cannot happen until human nature itself is changed by the molecular engineer. But we can profit from such knowledge in choosing between safe and perilous courses in life. There is one other requisite: We must first of all confess that we are not angels.

It is startling to witness the acceptance by sociobiology of this classical form of the Christian philosophy of history. Saint Augustine might quibble about some of the phraseology, but surely it would be hard for him to find anything in the preceding injunctions that differs from the essential message in his *City of God:* Man lives encumbered with a past, must confess his weakness, seek education in the ways of righteousness, and await salvation with hope and confidence.

It is, however, the failure of sociobiology to come to grips with the problem of cultural differences that sets up the major obstacle to cooperation with the human sciences, and this matter calls for special attention.

CHAPTER 4

HUMAN NATURE AND CULTURAL DIFFERENCES

If we look upon *Homo sapiens* as a unity, then the striking variety of culture elements and patterns among distinct populations from place to place and in the same populations from time to time obviously calls for explanation. This has been a persistent and central problem for the human sciences. It is of interest to social scientists, therefore, to see how biologists deal with the question, as it must be of concern to biologists to know how social scientists have dealt with it.

The matter of cultural differences might be of small import if we were confronted only with variations on themes—this item of courtship etiquette compared with another, one style of body ornament distinguished from another. Ethnographers probe this kind of detail and are sometimes chided for their devotion to trivia. That question aside, it should be apparent that there are observable differences among cultures that are by no means superficial. The life activities of people in England differ significantly from those of people in Iceland or in Sumatra or

in Nicaragua. Pastoral, agricultural, and industrial economies are not just stages in a continuum of "development"; they involve distinct life styles and contrasting
daily routines for persons. To say, again, that the culture
of the Romans in the second century differs only in degree from the culture of the Iroquois in the seventeenth
century or of Frenchmen in the twentieth is to make culture into a meaningless abstraction.

The significance and reality of cultural differences become clear when we view them as a set of actions and
their consequences. Seen as the historical experiences of
all peoples, so far as we can know them, cultural differences present us with an array of alternatives in
human activities. It is from an examination of histories in
this sense that we can become aware of the possibilities
in human social life.

Looked at in this way, the problem of cultural differences is one with the problem of cultural change, for
the question is how the differences have come to be as
they are, how the way of life of this people has come to
be different from the way of life of that other, or how the
culture of a given people at this time has come to differ
from its culture at an earlier time.

Cultural differences have been evaluated and explained variously. The approaches can be classified as
follows:

(1) Culture has been regarded, at one extreme, as the
expression of a universal human nature, and therefore, as
basically the same everywhere. From this point of view,
our proper object should be to discover, amidst insignificant differences, the similarities that underlie all cultures
and thus to reveal the nature of culture as such.

(2) At the other extreme, the various cultures of peo-

ples have been seen as singular outcomes of singular histories, each to be appreciated for its unique qualities, each the product of a special set of human attributes or of a fortuitous congeries of events.

(3) Or, while regarded as products of a uniform human nature, cultures have been described as partial expressions of that nature, each culture representing a degree of that expression achieved through time. Here, actual differences have been attributed to chance. (An interesting variation is the notion that some cultures—in extreme cases, all cultures—are reflections of a degenerated human nature. But theorists of progress since the seventeenth century have greatly outnumbered theorists of degeneration.)

(4) Cultural differences have been explained as expressions of racial differences, with a variety of accountings for racial diversity. Here an effort is made to associate cultural characteristics with physical attributes of populations, or with intervening psychological characteristics. In this category, as in the previous one, distinctions have been particularly invidious.

(5) Cultural differences have been described as products of differences in the physical environment. In its classical form, the idea was simply that elements in the environment directly shape populations in both their physical and cultural characteristics.

(6) In a quite distinct way, cultural differences can be viewed as adaptive responses to differences in the environment, with natural selection working on genetic variations to produce modified genotypes that have a significant relation to resulting modified cultures.

(7) In an important modification of (2), cultural differences have been classified and the classes explained

as outcomes of different types of historical experiences of the populations involved.

The kind of approach to cultural differences one chooses is a serious matter, both practically and theoretically. A search for universals through identification of similarities can take the form of prescribing the limits of culture, and so the boundaries of possible action. And a focus on similarities obviously tends to obscure the theoretical problem of cultural differences. Insistence on the absolute individuality of each culture can, on the other hand, create romantic visions of cultural destinies flowing from culture souls. In this case the methodological implication is that cultures are not comparable and that scientific knowledge about culture histories is not, therefore, possible. The alternatives lying between these extremes involve in some measure the difficulties of each.

A look at the history of some efforts to deal with the problem of cultural differences can help us to understand the current status of the inquiry, with particular reference to the recent contributions of sociobiologists.

When Westerners discovered a world new to them, a first reaction was wonder that there were peoples so different from themselves in both appearance and behavior. The early Greeks and Romans commonly sought to explain the differences they encountered in terms of physical environment. Climate, terrain, food, and other such features were taken to account for both biological and cultural differences. Color, body conformation, energy, disposition, and character were directly associated with quite specific meteorologic and geographic conditions, and cultural correlates of physical characteristics were noted in political, martial, and intellectual activities.[1]

Europeans who were later exposed to a broader and more striking range of human differences followed in this classical tradition. In the sixteenth century, Jean Bodin observed that both animals and men vary with climates and topographies, and that in men the variation extends to mental and moral qualities. Two centuries later, Montesquieu enlarged greatly on the same theme, and in the interval a rich literature on the subject had appeared.[2]

Concurrent with an environmental explanation of differences, Europeans in the sixteenth and seventeenth centuries entertained the beguiling idea that there are different kinds of human physiques and cultures simply because there are different kinds of people, and these kinds of people exist, not because of different physical environments, but because they are descended from different kinds of ancestors. This line of speculation appears to have been prompted chiefly by the discovery in America of men who could not, because of their "savage and brutish" appearance and customs, be regarded by some Europeans as descendants of Adam and Eve. Although the Church decreed that Indians had actually descended from the biblical pair, polygenist doctrine persisted in views that there had been separate creations before, after, or at the same time as the appearance of Adam. In some instances, the argument was rather detailed, turning on considerations of possible routes of human diffusion or on analysis of the distinctness of other animals besides man in the New World. In any event, the notion that there is a plurality of human races or kinds, with inherent differences sufficient to account for what appeared to be enormous cultural differences, was expressed as early as the sixteenth century.[3] There were occasional efforts in the seventeenth and early eighteenth centuries to classify people into separate races, based on physical characteristics, and to relate physical and cultural elements,[4] but full-scale and widespread racial theory was a nineteenth-century phenomenon.

The rejection of early efforts to explain cultural differences in terms of race or environment was a result, in part, of the fact that the explanations did not work. The problem of identifying races for this purpose has never been solved, and, more important perhaps, the way in which biological traits might manifest themselves in cultural traits—a mechanism by which this might come about—has been a largely neglected question. While the claims of physical environmentalists were usually more modest and better supported, it remained that histories of similar cultures in diverse environments, of different cultures in like environments, and of changing cultures in relatively stationary environments, rendered the extravagances of this school untenable. In addition, there was no doubt a reluctance in some quarters to accept such materialistic explanations of human affairs.

Where racial and environmental theories of differences have been discarded, however, the explanation does not lie entirely in either their feeble explanatory powers or in their moral implications. A peculiar tension between sensitivities to cultural similarities and to differences is characteristic of Western thought. When, in the eighteenth century, attention was focused on uniformity throughout nature, theories of cultural differences were neglected simply because the problem of differences itself was set aside.

Although Europeans were at first struck by the bewildering diversity of human form and custom revealed by the age of discovery, that reaction quite soon changed to an insistence on the similarity that underlay only apparent difference. The reasons for this shift in outlook are complex.

The tradition of classical learning was no doubt a powerful influence. Aristotle had sought to describe a world of nature made up of forms or kinds of eternal things. The object of science was to discover the real natures of these things and to distinguish them from aberrant or accidental representations observable in the actual world. Variations within a type—in the political state, for instance—were regarded, then, as abnormalities or, at least, inconsequential nuances. It was, of course, of utmost importance to distinguish the pure form and not confuse it with deviations. At the same time, however, the coming to be of instances of the forms was depicted as a process of change marked by stages that represented degrees of perfection achieved by the thing changing. Besides monstrous or accidental departures from the pure type, therefore, variations were observable also in normal stages of growth approaching a defined end. And, again, it was necessary to distinguish between these signs of mere immaturity and indications of abnormality.[5] In any case, the object of inquiry was to discriminate among diversities and to identify unity.

In medieval thought, as we have noted in another context, an emphasis on the search for unity continued. The theory of microcosms and macrocosms was essentially a statement about similar principles operating at corresponding levels throughout the universe, so that discovery of a pattern or process at one place in the fabric of existence could be taken as a sure clue to what would be found elsewhere. This image was associated with the concept of a chain of being or a great hierarchy of entities of such finely graduated diversity that the whole formed a unity in which any single item was connected to all others by a sequence of similarities.

The seventeenth and eighteenth centuries saw this belief in unity prevail over the first impression of diversity following Europe's acquaintance with alien peoples. Universalism, or uniformitarianism—expressed now in terms of laws of nature that operate in the same economical way throughout time and space—seemed to be in keeping with the new science that had revealed a similitude of motions on earth and in the heavens. In fact, science could be defined as the detection of hitherto undiscovered commonness among phenomena previously regarded as idiosyncratic.

Apart from this formal consideration, Europeans welcomed a perspective from which the awful outlandishness of new tribes beyond the seas could be moderated by detection of fundamental likenesses to themselves. The unfamiliar was explained by assimilating it to the familiar. The sense of comfort and satisfaction so gained was well expressed by Daniel Defoe when his hero, so recently aghast at the horror of cannibalism among the Caribs, comes to observe in Friday "the same powers, the same reason, the same affections, the same sentiments of kindness and obligation, the same passions and resentments of wrongs, the same sense of gratitude, sincerity, fidelity, and all the capacities of doing good, and receiving good" that God bestowed on "us."[6] And so Turgot, with mock dismay: "Alas! Our fathers . . . resembled the American savages!"[7]

The early modern European preoccupation with cultural similarities involved, on the one hand, an attempt to discover the natural in the universal and thus to lay a firm basis for an absolute and common morality. This was a perilous and uncertain task, because different searches for universals yielded different finds. "The natural" proved to be an elusive and problematic thing.[8] Similar difficulties plagued efforts to determine the common among the diverse in culture, apart from the moral question, for the counting and measuring necessary to this task was a challenging undertaking seldom even attempted. The temptation to identify one's own society as the bearer of normal culture was powerful under such circumstances.

Cultural similarities were pursued at this time also, as we have seen, with a view to reconstructing culture history. This procedure depended on identification of similarities between cultures—in the first instance, similarities between existing savage peoples and what was known of ancient Europeans, and then, successively, similarities that linked each member of the progressive series to its neighbors. In the nineteenth century, this arsenal of likenesses was further supplied by attempts to identify survivals of savagery in civilized society and thus to establish a time link between basically similar entities.

Obviously, however, this use of similarities did leave a world of differences to be pondered. European progress theorists were not, after all, likely to carry their search for universals too far. Civilization had arisen, to be sure, out of savagery, but a civilized man was something quite different from a savage. Europeans were one people in a family of nations, but they were regarded as a very special people. The question remained as to why radical differences in degrees of polish or civilization among peoples existed at any given time.

The common reply of progress theorists in the eighteenth and nineteenth centuries was that differences resulted from accidents. While similar causes worked uniformly for gradual advance, interruptions in the form of war, pestilence, bad political rule, and the like were to be expected. Also, adverse physical environments hindered the progress of some peoples. It was even possible that some tribes or nations suffered enfeebled faculties that limited their capacity for progress.[9] Progress, to put the matter in familiar Aristotelian terms, was what happened if nothing interfered; but interference there was, for things came to be not only by rule but by accident.

So, it turned out that Europeans confronted with a fascinating world of cultural differences attributed them to chance. Faced with the questions of how peoples shaped their lives in different ways and how the consequences for Europeans compared with the consequences for others, Europeans called it a willy-nilly process and retreated with the smug judgment that, whatever the cause, they had come out on top. As Auguste Comte put it early in the nineteenth century, cultural differences exist *par des causes quelconques,* and it is fortunate that something had operated to delay the progress of other peoples since that affords us the means to reconstruct the course of our own advance.[10] It is tragic that a people who were afforded an unprecedented opportunity to extend horizons by comparative historical inquiry instead so generally denied the plurality of histories and restricted their vision to a single, universal history proceeding to a single end.

But now, if human cultures are all basically alike, and the process of cultural change is uniform, similarity itself must be explained. The obvious monogenist answer to this question was that similarity is to be expected, given the unity of the human race. The matter was not left there, however, for an attempt was made to specify just what the unity of the race consisted in and how the elements of the unity were expressed in corresponding social and cultural phenomena. These elements of the unity have been referred to traditionally as human nature, and, as noted earlier, a common procedure has been to seek an explanation of the social and cultural as a product of human nature. When Aristotle found man to be by nature a political animal the object was to account for (and to justify) the political state as a widespread social institution.

There is an attractive simplicity to this procedure. Mandeville, satirizing the thought of his eighteenth-century contemporaries, duly noted that there is "not a more copious nor a more faithful Volume than human Nature," and advocated its diligent perusal for revelation of the "hidden Spring, that gives Life and Motion," to all human actions. It is much easier, he pointed out, to account for the character of a society in this way than to bother about what had happened in history.

When I have a Mind to dive into the Origin of any Maxim or political Invention, for the use of Society in general, I don't trouble my Head with enquiring after the Time or Country, in which it was first heard of, nor what others have wrote or said about it; but I go directly to the Fountain Head, human Nature itself, and look for the Frailty or Defect in Man, that is reme-dy'd or supply'd by that Invention: When Things are very ob-scure, I sometimes make Use of Conjectures to find my Way.[11]

Not only was the complicated and confusing and unruly mass of historical details thus to be avoided, but one could proceed with assurance that one was dealing with essentials, with a set of bases from which all significant results flow, with the real and ultimate sources or pro-ducers of what is truly pan-human.

As Mandeville said, things could be obscure in this sort of enterprise, and it is interesting to observe the in-genuity of early human-nature theorists in discovering qualities in human nature that suited their various pur-poses. Thomas Hobbes found in man a fear and utter sel-fishness that demanded creation of a powerful ruling body. John Locke, with more moderate political ends in view, saw in human beings a capacity for social life that Hobbes had denied them. Throughout the eighteenth century human-nature study was pursued in a serious and painstaking effort to make it the basis of a science of man and society. The aim was to find out what men gen-erally do and do not do, to discover what is "natural" to man. In retrospect, however, it is clear that this "proper study of Mankind" consisted essentially of putting into the vessel, human nature, sets of qualities, propensities, instincts, drives, or tendencies that could be shown to produce sets of results that had already been gleaned from casual historical observation or were desiderata in the ethical views of the investigator. So, Adam Smith, in the presence of a particular form of the division of labor, which he saw as a product of natural history, and observing a certain kind of marketplace behavior in his countrymen, explained the division of labor as the result of a propensity in mankind to truck, barter, and exchange. Adam Ferguson, contemplating the history of a busy European people in the midst of a flurry of technical invention, endowed humanity with an innate tendency to be always changing and improving its ways.[12]

The underlying purpose of these eighteenth- and early nineteenth-century studies, it should be recalled, was discovery of a universal ethic solidly based in human nature. "Moral philosophers," as they were known, sought regularity and rule in nature not just for intellectual ordering of chaos but for guidance to principles of human conduct that are in keeping with what human beings really are. It would be misleading to suppose that these scholars were content to seek morality in scripture or in casuistry. They sought it in science.

The most striking and influential example of this endeavor is Jeremy Bentham's *An Introduction to the Principles of Morals and Legislation* (1780). Adopting the axiom that any humanistic study with moral and practical objectives must begin with a statement of what man is, the great utilitarian declared, with somewhat self-conscious arbitrariness, that man is governed by twin masters, pleasure and pain. He seeks to enhance his chances for pleasure and minimize the likelihood of pain. Nothing else moves him. He has not the slightest inherent inclination to society with his fellows, although reason can show him some identity of interests with others and he can be induced by sanctions to behave as if he shared interests with others. In reality, however, there are, according to Bentham, only individuals in the human world; groups or societies are fictions. This is because only individuals feel pleasure or pain; a "number" of people might experience pleasure in the sense of there being a "greatest good for the greatest number," but what would appear to be a group phenomenon here is no more than a sum of individual feelings.

Bentham's prime purpose was to arrive at a sound ethic, a realistic ethic based not on philosophic or theological cant, but on a rigorous analysis of man's nature conducted in accord with canons of the recently triumphant physical sciences. He scorned the systems of ethical philosophers who deduced moral principles from unsupported first principles or postulated imperatives. He was outraged especially by those who endowed man with angelic qualities of selflessness and concern for others while the evidence was clear that every human being acted solely in his own interest. Calculation of amounts of pleasure and of pain, of intensities and durations of each, of pain in deferred pleasure and pleasure in deferred pain, and a host of such qualities and their quantitative relationships received Bentham's careful attention. He was, indeed, engaged in a "felicific calculus," and he was ever mindful of the fact that human nature was everywhere the same and that his moral principles were therefore as applicable in Hindustan as in France.[13]

The methods used in this quest for what man is, ranged from the avowed introspection of Hobbes ("read thyself") to the fairly refined psychology of Adam Ferguson. But human-nature theorists encountered a methodological dilemma. They could not, after all, "look into" human nature and see anything like springs to action. They found it difficult, we have seen, to compare men with animals without merely reading into animals preexistent ideas about human behavior. What they were actually doing was gathering, as best they could, information about the typical ways people had acted in classes of situations and then attributing the actions to propensities to act those ways. In the case of Bentham and most others, the information came, at best, from unsystematic observation of fellow countrymen in their daily activities. (Bentham said, if you do not believe that people act to gain pleasure and avoid pain, go and look at them.) David Hume suggested a more disciplined approach when he argued that the chief use of history is

only to discover the constant and universal principles of human nature, by showing men in all varieties of circumstances and situations, and furnishing us with materials from which we may form our observations and become acquainted with the regular springs of human action and behaviour.[14]

If what we actually observe, however, are circumstances and situations and regularly associated human action and behavior, and that is all, then reference to human nature has no other function than giving names to actions and behaviors that occur under designated conditions. If men are observed to act with characteristic aggression in typical situations of stress, nothing is added by way of explanation when we say that men are by nature aggressive. We would know, Hume seems to be saying, that men are by nature aggressive only by virtue of our having observed them acting aggressively at certain times. Traditional human-nature study failed to deal satisfactorily with this impasse, and the problem remains, we shall note, with current human-nature theorists.

In the formal shaping of anthropology and sociology in the nineteenth century the problem of cultural differences was generally neglected, and human-nature study also took a secondary position in the great effort to establish a positive science of man. The influence of Auguste Comte in both of these areas was decisive.

Arguing against ambitious attempts then being made to derive social science from physiology, Comte maintained that it is impossible to reconstruct or predict the course of human history from a knowledge of general laws of human nature. It is quite true, he granted, that human progress flows from human organization, that progress results from the "instinctive tendency of the human race to perfect itself." Whatever generalizations we reach about development or progress, therefore, must be checked against and brought into accord with what we know about the nature of man. But we cannot deduce a law of progress from principles of human nature because human nature is modified in the succession of generations. There are, indeed, universal tendencies of human nature, but these basic elements are shaped and modified, Comte believed, in the course of universal history.[15] The circularity in so much of eighteenth-century human-nature theory was thus averted.

Comte, a firm believer in the fixity of species, was not suggesting anything like a Darwinian evolution of man. All that the human race had achieved and would achieve existed as established potential in the first man. And yet he was clearly implying that if we look about us at peoples in various stages of social and cultural progress, we shall find them differently constituted—they have different human natures. Comte had vague doubts about the capability of some peoples for unassisted advance, but he saw the generality of men fit for progress, and he certainly did not regard civilization as a racial phenomenon. Although Comte did not dwell on the point, it appears that he was suggesting that a change in human nature accompanies a change in society, but that the former is a result of the latter.

This would seem to be the position of Lewis Henry Morgan, later in the century. For Morgan, savage and barbarous peoples have "inferior mental endowments," but they have the same brain as civilized man. It is just that the civilized brain has "grown older and larger with the experience of the ages." Some of the "excrescences" of civilization are to be viewed as mental atavisms, relics not yet eradicated from the human brain. Although Morgan spoke on occasion of natural selection in the progress of human social institutions, he tended to view advance as a product of effort, or "unconscious effort," in choosing among alternatives revealed by experience. A larger brain would thus be both a product of and a producer of civilization, but brain growth would result from use.[16]

Marx and Engels in similar fashion recognized important differences in the nature of apes and men and in the nature of men before and after their experience in the labor process. Engels noticed a complicated interaction between cultural (labor, tools, speech) and biological (brain, hands, erect posture) factors in human history, and he believed that there were differences in degree of development among existing peoples resulting from the process. But there was no suggestion in Engels' consideration of this matter that superior physical endowment either initiated the process or, in itself, explained various contemporary levels of development.[17]

In general, then, the enthusiasm for human-nature analysis that prevailed in eighteenth-century scholars waned among their nineteenth-century successors. Comte, Morgan, and Engels saw human society as dependent, of course, on the presence of human beings. And they regarded cultural change as connected, in a general way, with biological change. Yet, those observations were quite incidental to their systems. They did not derive specific social institutions from specific traits of human nature, nor did they try to explain specific cultural changes as results of specific biological changes. Their conception of the relationship of the cultural and biological was so limited, and so vague, that it might better be said that they accepted man as a biological entity, recognized the importance of that given, and then proceeded on a social and cultural level to seek explanations of sociocultural phenomena. Man's nature could no longer be comfortably viewed as basic to sociocultural phenomena when it was seen, most significantly, as a changing result of sociocultural history.

The tendency to seek human nature in human history was not, however, accompanied by any widespread effort to explain cultural differences in strictly historical terms. Comte thought that there was a law of progress that rigorously determined the successive states through which the human race must pass in its general development. The substance of that law was formulated by Comte from a philosophic view of human history, not from an interpretation of human nature. In any event, his attention focused on the course of development, and different historical or existing societies represented for him stages or steps in a universal evolutionary process. The emphasis was thus on unity or similarities, and differences were set aside as irrelevant consequences of chance occurrences or abnormal situations. Morgan was also convinced that "corresponding" institutions were observable among the American aborigines on the one hand and ancient Greeks and Romans on the other, and that the principal institutions of all mankind had been developed from "a few primary germs of thought," guided by a "natural logic of the human mind" common to all because it was an attribute of the brain itself. Morgan did not, however, connect specific germs or logic with specific social and cultural elements, and the emphasis again was on the law of progress itself. So, too, the occasional inclination of Marx to see iron laws working inexorably to bring about uniform results in the economic history of all nations rested on a conviction that a dialectic in history was responsible, rather than on an image of a common human nature expressing itself.[18]

In the magnificent nineteenth-century humanist undertaking to depict the evolution or development of human society, human culture, and every separate social institution and culture element, the idea of progress or development guided the interpretation of cultural similarities and differences. Problems special to a concern with similarities arose. If cultural differences are to be used as stages in constructing a generalized culture history, and if this can be done only on the assumption that all cultures have similar histories, then it seemed important to know if any given similarities are really a manifestation of whatever produces culture histories as such, or if they are only a result of one people borrowing cultural items from another or of two or more peoples deriving their cultures in whole or part from the same ancestral culture. Similarities that were to be taken as signs of something culturally inherent had to be distinguished from the other two kinds.[19] The prospect of tracing out complicated and divergent lines of contact and descent among myriad peoples in order to account for their conditions did not appeal to minds dedicated to uniformity and universalism. One could easily forget the very quest for unity in such an enterprise.

And something of the sort actually occurred. As the facts of cultural contact and derivation became more generally acknowledged,[20] diffusion as a process in itself attracted increasing attention and a lively dispute went on in anthropology between evolutionists and diffusionists. This argument continued to confine attention to cultural similarities, with the usual neglect of the problem of differences. Similarities could be sought as evidence of diffusion as well as for the purpose of supporting independent and unilinear development.

Excesses of both schools led to serious questioning of such theoretical orientations for anthropology, and many anthropologists resolved to divorce themselves from such controversy and go about the proper business of describing, with due attention to structure and function, the social arrangements and cultural artifacts of the non-European peoples with whom the discipline had been traditionally concerned.[21] Social and cultural evolutionism became generally discredited, while diffusionist studies, under the influence of Franz Boas, became specialized efforts to trace continuities in the distribution of culture elements for the purpose of discovering historical connections among peoples. An historical perspective has since been used with encouraging results in the area of cultural differences, as we shall have occasion to note. But modern anthropologists and sociologists have devoted themselves mainly to structural and functional analysis, to a search for basic and enduring characteristics of societies and cultures, and to the question of how social equilibrium is achieved, maintained, and restored. The problem of persistence has taken precedence over the problem of change, the identification and explanation of similarities over the problem of differences.[22]

It should be recalled at this point, however, that during the great nineteenth-century effort to discover a law of progress, or of evolution, in the cultural history of man, there was a strong revival in European thought of the notion that cultural differences are consequences of racial—that is, biological—differences among geographically distinct human populations. Historians of race theory convincingly explain this resurgence by pointing out that it was only when slavery and the exploitation or extermination of non-European peoples became widespread and suspect that justification of such activity was called for. The idea that there are innately inferior and innately superior peoples served to rationalize Europe's relationship with the rest of the world.[23]

To European scholars who had concluded that like minds under like conditions had produced a world of cultural similarities, the idea that different *kinds* of people produce different cultures was upsetting. It was not difficult for Comte or Morgan to acknowledge that different conditions of human nature accompanied successive stages in social evolution, but an assertion that these were not stages in a universal process at all, but stark consequences of there being different populations of culture producers, had serious implications. Cultural differences could be regarded as differences of degree in a uniform development only on the premise of human unity, with equal cultural potential in all populations. Then actual cultural differences could be attributed to

111

accidental retardations of development, and the differences could be used to represent stages in the process of cultural evolution.

Racial explanation of cultural diversity was also repugnant to scholars who considered themselves rid of the habit of deducing history from analysis of human nature. The renewed argument that human societies could be understood as biological products came at just the time when many European thinkers believed they had exposed that error and were engaged in distinctively social explanation of the social.[24]

The new racial theories began their appearance before Darwin's inquiry into the value of human races in 1871. Darwin's suggestion that natural selection had worked variously in geographically distinct human populations to render some more biologically capable of civilization than others would appear to be a novel factor in the situation. The reaction of humanistic scholars to this proposition is not clear-cut. Darwin's own ambiguous position on biological and cultural transmission of capabilities is no doubt partly responsible for the confusion. The atmosphere was also clouded by identification of the Darwinian picture of struggle and selection with traditional laissez-faire social theory. "Social Darwinism" employed Darwinian terminology, but only at the level of analogy.[25] Darwin's use of words taken from the common language of humanist discourse encouraged a fairly common belief that, so far as human history is concerned, he was simply talking about contests between individuals or groups in which some won and some lost, with a resulting domination of the losers by the winners, or, more abstractly, that he referred to the way in which certain ideas or implements or procedures came to prevail over or take the place of others by virtue of their greater serviceability or utility. There was nothing new in this to chroniclers of human wars, economic competitions, and other forms of rivalry. They were moved, at best, only to remark how strikingly such familiar features of human history had been found by Darwin to prevail throughout nature.[26]

Yet the message about human races in *The Descent of Man* was clear and compelling in certain respects. Darwin had observed that, from the point of view of descent with modification, the monogenist-polygenist dispute is irrelevant. As man began to emerge from an ancestral form shared with other primates, a number of geographically separate human populations were formed. Individuals comprising these various "tribes or nations" were, as collectivities, shaped differently in both bodily form and mental attributes by the action of sexual and natural selection in different given environments. Races, then, are not to be regarded as true breeding descendants of different original stocks. Races, if one wishes to use that term, are simply the array of differently adapted human populations at a point in time. These adaptations, as Darwin judged them, are by no means of equal value, nor are they random. There is a tendency (Darwin said) nay, a necessity (Spencer said) for populations to improve their adaptation, and for the progress to continue indefinitely, although degree of progress differs among populations. The more progressive societies would, however, in the inevitable course of events, destroy backward societies, who might otherwise have succeeded in the long journey of adaptation if they had developed sufficient numbers of individuals with capacities requisite to civilization.

This picture of social and cultural change in human

populations could achieve substance only if a measure of adaptation was found and if a connection between the measure and hereditary traits was specified. When Darwin spoke of the traits in human beings that fitted them for progress—traits, therefore, that signified adaptation—he took for granted the physical qualities that gave them a relative advantage in reproduction. He was clear about the way in which such traits facilitated reproduction, and he was clear about the way in which such traits increased in succeeding generations. It is here that explanation in Darwin's theory is so powerful as to border on the obvious. When, however, he spoke of the individual moral, intellectual, and social traits that characterized civilized or progressive societies, he was neither precise nor obvious.[27] Darwin did little more at this point than enumerate the qualities that he admired in his own people and express his conviction that behavior flowing from such qualities was responsible for advanced society, that is, a society like his own. When it came to a specification of the way these moral and social traits were passed on from one generation to the next or how their extent or intensity increased, he was uncertain and equivocal. He did not deny the importance of what we now call socialization and cultural tradition. He was aware that the success of a progressive people depended on its numbers and its superior physical and intellectual qualities, but how these three factors were related and in what proportions relative to degrees of success were questions quite unsettled in his mind. He was bothered by the evidence, in his own and other societies, of a tendency for "inferior" members to increase at a faster rate than the "better." He recognized that it is very difficult to account for any actual case of progress, and that it depends not just on the operation of natural selection but on a complication of favorable circumstances. Darwin did not attempt to discover those circumstances. He argued only that the presence of able men is a necessity—a given, as it were, in the situation—and that ability has an organic basis that is selected for.[28]

The fact that humanists could not find in Darwin clues to the puzzle of cultural differences is understandable. Now it is necessary to inquire whether sociobiological theory might be more serviceable in explanation of human cultural differences.

One must be struck at once by the persistence among sociobiologists of the eighteenth-century search for universals and concern with cultural similarities. The objective, according to Edward O. Wilson, is to identify "human qualities . . . insofar as they appear to be general traits of the species," and then to connect "social traits occurring through all cultures" with their corresponding genetic bases in the "human type." Wilson urges recognition of the fact that the social behavior of humans cannot be shaped into just any form, because a hereditary component determines certain limits. "Genetic constraints and the restricted number of environments in which human beings can live limit the array of possible outcomes substantially."[29]

Durkheim and Radcliffe-Brown are said to have been mistaken, therefore, when they sought the dynamics of culture in culture itself, for culture is only a statistical product of the behavior of human beings, and there are strong genetic controls on human behavior. While there is such a thing as cultural evolution, then, it cannot run contrary to biological evolution for long. Natural selection and genetic constraint see to it that "cultural mimicry" of real biological adaptation stays within limits. "The genes hold culture on a leash."[30]

The fact that there is such a thing as human nature, formed in some significant degree by natural selection and thus containing genetic components, explains, this argument continues, the substantial uniformity observable across all human societies and cultures. Cultural change has been limited to certain pathways by human nature. It should be expected, then, that "emergence of civilization has everywhere followed a definable sequence." And that is said to be the case. Although genetic changes cannot account for most of the concrete cultural changes resulting in civilization, the genetic influence has been sufficient to produce major similarities among the early civilizations of Egypt, Mesopotamia, India, China, Mexico, and Central and South America—similarities that cannot otherwise be explained by diffusion or chance. The similar aggressive activities of all peoples in all times are also explicable, according to Wilson, as results of the genetic makeup of human nature. A nearly universal subordination of women to men is also a consequence of a slight but uniform genetic difference between the sexes.[31] And so on. Human cultures are alike because human beings are alike.

It appears, then, that sociobiologists have chosen quite deliberately to center their attention on cultural similarities. As Irven DeVore has put it, they are simply interested more in what is universally human than in what is culturally variable. That is not, however, only a matter of taste. Wilson says that it is "not nearly so important" to notice that women in some societies are virtual slaves and in others are almost equals of men as it is to notice that there is, apparently, a slight genetic difference that makes women less assertive and physically aggressive than men. DeVore agrees that different cultures produce "only minor variations on the theme of the species," while "Almost everything that's importantly human— including behavioral flexibility—is universal, and developed in the context of our shared genetic background." [32]

Whether or not sociobiologists succeed in demonstrating that cultural similarities are genetically explicable, the consequences of this general position for the study of differences deserve notice. The fact of cultural differences is, of course, undeniable. [33] What, then, is to be made of them? In meeting this question, sociobiologists take the same general position as classical social evolutionists: the differences are of degree. But whereas the evolutionists saw them as differences of degree of development or progress, sociobiologists tend to see them, as DeVore puts it, as variations on a given theme. Similarly, Wilson says that the important thing about the evolution of culture is that it has created a situation (for civilized people, at any rate) in which human nature is no longer suited to the demands of social and cultural life. From that point of view, differences among cultures represent the relatively insignificant fact that the cultural element in the clash between human nature and culture takes on a variety of outward forms.

The question of cultural alternatives in the lives of peoples now becomes a matter of judging the fit of a culture to a given human nature. [34] Variations of that fit do not signify. A capacity for culture has evolved in man, but it is a capacity for "one culture or another," and anything that is in accord with man's biology is suitable.

117

The cultures of societies move along "one or the other" of a "set" of evolutionary paths marked out by a genetic human nature.[35] Which path is of import only by virtue of the biological fit or its lack.

Human culture histories here emerge as fortuitous meanderings of people within bounds set by a human nature produced by organic evolution. Thus the capacity for altruistic behavior is said to have evolved by selection, although it is strongly influenced by the "vagaries" of cultural evolution. The biological evidence of sex differences at birth suggests, again, that the universality of a sexual division of labor is not an "accident" of cultural evolution. In the same fashion, the determinants of human aggression are genetic, environmental, and the "accidental details that contribute to cultural drift," as seen in "the previous history of the group, which biasses it toward the adoption of one cultural innovation as opposed to another." Human cultural differences do not imply choices among significant alternatives. That would apparently introduce a scientifically unmanageable element of free will—"we are biological and our souls cannot fly free."[36]

A difficulty for sociobiology arises in this context. If culture histories are in themselves superficial phenomena, and if cultural differences are to be regarded as products of these histories, how shall we account for the striking differences between hunter-gatherer and civilized industrial societies? Are those, too, but surface differences to be explained by the fact that "ethnographic detail is genetically underprescribed"? If human social evolution is "obviously more cultural than genetic," and, if it is true that human populations do not differ very much genetically,[37] is there not a crucial question to be answered in cultural rather than genetic terms—the question of how the obviously significant culture differences today have come to be as they are?

Humanists are understandably concerned about that question, and their concern about sociobiology's response to it should be understood. If foundations for cultural similarities are sought in biological universals, then an expectation is fostered that bases for cultural differences be looked for in biological particulars. The sociobiological response to this situation is equivocal. Wilson has said that, while it is "conventional wisdom" that cultural variation is phenotypic rather than genetic in origin, it is extreme environmentalism to say that there is no genetic variance in the transmission of culture—i.e., to say that the *capacity* for culture is transmitted by a single human genotype.

Although the genes have given away most of their sovereignty, they maintain a certain amount of influence in at least the behavioral qualities that underlie variations between cultures. . . . Even a small portion of this variance invested in population differences might predispose societies toward cultural differences. At the very least, we should try to measure this amount.[38]

In pursuing the question, Wilson has observed that while there is "little evidence of genetic variation in social behavior *within* the human species," how much variation there might be is an "important but delicate question," and "the evidence is strong that a substantial fraction of human behavioral variation is based on genetic differences among individuals." In his opinion, existing information has reduced the psychic unity of mankind from a dogma to a testable hypothesis.[39]

Wilson asks us to look at man as a conventional animal

species so far as genetic variation affecting behavior is concerned. The inference is that varieties or subspecies might be designated in this respect. When he candidly raises the question of racial differences in behavior, he states:

The evidence is strong that almost all differences between human societies are based on learning and social conditioning rather than on heredity. And yet perhaps not quite all. . . . populations are to some extent genetically diverse in the physical and mental properties underlying social behavior.[40]

Variation in the rules [of behavior] among human cultures, however slight, might provide clues to underlying genetic differences, particularly when it is correlated with variation in behavioral traits known to be heritable.[41]

On the other hand, in speaking of altruistic behavior, Wilson says that it is only the "underlying emotion" that evolved through the genes; the form and intensity of altruistic acts are to a large extent culturally determined.

Human social evolution is obviously more cultural than genetic. . . . The sociobiological hypothesis does not therefore account for differences among societies, but it can explain why human beings differ from other mammals and why, in one narrow aspect, they more closely resemble social insects.[42]

The apparent ambiguity in all of this might be resolved, in part, by seeking to explain cultural differences as variations representing adaptations to different environments.[43] This would require a delineation of human subspecies, varieties, populations, or races identifiable by their different activities—their cultural works—in somewhat the same way systematists can distinguish varieties of other animal species by differences in behavioral patterns. This is distinct, of course, from the sort of environmentalism that Bodin or Montesquieu or some modern geographers have espoused. And it would be quite different from merely taking notice of how various circumstances can shape or guide a common genetic disposition so as to produce minor variations on universal behavioral themes. Variations in the opportunistic activities of certain species are evidently not taken by systematists as bases for identifying subspecies, nor are adjustments by phenotypes to passing circumstances confused with adaptations of genotypes to relatively stable environmental conditions. If cultural differences among human populations are taken seriously, if they are accorded a significance only equal to traits used to distinguish varieties in other species, if they are seen as something more than merely "one or another" way of doing the same thing, and if we seek to be clear and specific about biological foundations of human cultures, then an identification of genetically distinguishable human subspecies or varieties would seem to be in order.

Or, equivocation might be avoided by adopting Darwin's sole clue to explaining the difference between one society and another: difference in "the number of men endowed with high intellectual and moral faculties, as well as . . . their standard of excellence."[44]

It can hardly fail to impress humanists who have struggled with the problem of cultural differences that Darwin made no attempt to distinguish actual cultures on the basis of such criteria. He only asserted that his own culture was highest and therefore, presumably, had the largest number of highly endowed men. And he could see no way of explaining why one society rather than another produced a larger number of such men.

Modern sociobiologists do not follow up on this Darwinian clue. Nor do they undertake in any systematic way to associate variations among cultures with a corresponding array of human varieties. Remarks about different "adaptive responses" or "underlying genetic differences" or a "certain amount" of genetic influence in the production of behavioral differences contribute little to even a clarification of the problem. In the presence of such vagueness, Wilson's comparatively forthright declarations that human social evolution is more cultural than genetic, that sociobiology does not account for differences among societies, and that "almost all" differences among human societies derive from socialization processes, must suggest to humanists that there is at least a substantial range of variation out there that biologists are not going to explain. A perspective that yields, essentially, the observation that cultural differences are there because, and to the extent that, a genetic compulsion to uniformity is lacking, offers little positive direction to inquiry aimed at an understanding of the sources and implications of the range of life possibilities so far experienced by man.

Bound, then, by its preoccupation with cultural universals deriving from the uniformity of human nature, sociobiology appears to offer little more to students of cultural differences than they have found in their heritage of eighteenth-century human-nature theory.

CHAPTER 5

HISTORY AND CULTURAL DIFFERENCES

Eighteenth- and nineteenth-century European devotion to the idea of progress, development, or evolution of human society was widespread, but it was not all-encompassing. There were scholars who worked in a separate tradition. Their attention was focused on the problem of cultural differences, and they stood outside the school of thought that explained cultural differences in terms of biological differences. It is a serious mistake to characterize this group of inquirers as antievolutionists or as radical environmentalists, for that is to misrepresent their views and to overlook the positive features of their work. Instead of attributing cultural variety to either constitutional differences or to chance events, these thinkers sought an explanation in comparison of the histories of peoples. They accepted those histories as comparable and believed that the comparison could yield generalizations about specific kinds of human experiences and activities. This chapter will present examples of this type of inquiry and examine the relevance of biology to it.

A striking eighteenth-century illustration of the historical approach to differences is provided in the work of David Hume. Human-nature theorist though he was, Hume believed that different "national characters" cannot be accounted for by physical causes. He was unusually sensitive to the fact that nations differ in their achievements in the arts and sciences. This he attributed to different historical experience, not to an uneven distribution of genius among peoples. In particular, he noted that interruptions of the traditional order are preludes to progress in learning. In this connection he suggested that contact and intercourse between diverse peoples are common settings for such disruption, but any influence, he believed, that interferes with the ordinary course of life in a community can open new paths of thought or force a search for solutions to new problems created by breakdown of routine. It is noteworthy that Hume saw no point in pressing for an ultimate source of differences beyond the variety of historical experience. History had to be explained in its own terms and not as heaps of incomprehensible chance occurrences of only secondary importance.[1]

A similar perspective is evident in a series of remarkable essays written by James Dunbar in 1781. Dunbar, a professor of philosophy at King's College and the University of Aberdeen, began with Hume's conviction that the various levels of achievement reached by peoples call for explanation and are not accounted for by relative genius or capacity. The biological explanation was carefully considered, but Dunbar tried to demonstrate that constitutional differences among peoples are "fluctuating and contingent." When the causes of civilization are so various and so complex, he argued, we can draw no conclusions about the "relative capacity" of peoples by the stage they occupy at any given time. He concluded, with language still common in the debate today, that "the genius of man is so flexible, so open to impressions from without, so susceptible of early culture, that between hereditary, innate, and acquired propensities, it is hard to draw the line of distinction." Dunbar did not assert the absolute equality of all races. (Even Hume had doubts about the Negro.) They might well have breathed, at first, "unequal proportions of the aetherial spirit," or have been variously shaped by the external elements. But the "capital distinctions" among the tribes, he believed, flow from causes subsequent to birth.

Those causes, he ventured, are to be sought in the histories of peoples, in the records of their activities. The doings of human beings differ with their various circumstances and experiences, not with their natures. Dunbar sought to show that development of the arts and sciences depends on free intercourse among men, which in turn is a consequence of a republican form of government. Progress demands a "concurrence of such various causes" that decline or stagnation have been at least as common for want of such a "contexture of events." It seemed probable to him, therefore, that barbarous nations become civilized usually as a result of contact with civilization, and that civilization might have arisen independently in only a few cases, and perhaps only once.[2]

Hume and Dunbar were clearly aware, then, of the problem of differences and looked for solutions in historical terms. If their explanations tended to generality or vagueness, they were to be succeeded by others who pressed the question. Hugh Murray, in 1808, became explicit about the causes of progress—about why some na-

125

tions advanced and others did not, thus producing the array of differences before us.

The point of departure was acceptance of Johann Friedrich Blumenbach's thesis on the basic unity of the human race. Blumenbach had resisted biological explanation of differences in achievement with the dry observation that it is always easier to name new species of men than it is to account for human variety.[3] So Murray rejected the notion that variation in moral and intellectual endowment could explain progress or its lack. He was aware, of course, that peoples differ greatly in external characteristics, and he believed only that they were "altogether, or very nearly" the same in intellect and morality. The point was that differences in natural endowment could not account for the extreme differences in achievement among contemporary peoples or in the same people from time to time.

Murray designated four positive and two negative conditions of progress. The positive are population density, free communication among different societies and among different members of the same society, accumulation of wealth, and "great public events." The negative conditions are actually the obverse of two of the positive—freedom from an oppressive necessity of labor and freedom from coercion. Murray supported his thesis with limited evidence that these conditions had prevailed in the classic ages of cultural efflorescence in Athens, Rome, Florence, and Britain. Of particular interest, however, is his argument that progress is not a natural or normal process. People must be roused out of their customary "torpid and inactive" state, and this can be done, he said, only when exposures to alien ideas and customs "free the mind from the chains of inveterate habit." Such exposure is the result of "public commotions." Most of these "great public events" are wars.[4]

Although Murray's discussion is cast in the prevailing mold of the idea of progress, the various degrees of progress (as he saw cultural differences) caught his attention and called for explanation. That is a marked departure from the progress theorists' view that differences are effects of accidental, secondary, or proximate causes.

A concern with cultural differences, once a biological explanation was rejected, involved thinkers like Murray in a pluralist conception of history. Instead of taking observed differences as given and arranging them in a series to represent stages in a universal process of culture growth, the different kinds of cultures themselves are recognized as products of kinds of histories. Universal history, or the development of Mankind or of any other hypostatized entity appears as an abstraction that only obscures the basic problem of differences.

This conception of human experience as a collection of histories was clearly expressed in mid-nineteenth century by the English jurist, scholar, and statesman, George Cornewall Lewis. Influenced by the German school of historical criticism, Lewis turned away from one of the favorite ideas of the Enlightenment: he denied the existence of a society of the entire human race and he denied, therefore, the occurrence of a universal history of society. The history of the human race, he maintained, is only the aggregate of the histories of the several communities into which people have been divided. To abstract from those histories in search of a scientific unity would create only a mirage if the individual differences of community experiences are disregarded. This did not mean, to Lewis, that scholarship must limit itself to an appreci-

127

ation of distinct and unique little histories. The histories of nations, he observed, intersect and influence one another. And there are, indeed, common features in histories. But what must be avoided, if social science is to be anything more than a conceptual arranging of types, is an attempt to reduce a profusion of histories to a single line.[5]

Lewis arrived at no comprehensive historical theory of social and cultural diversity and was, in fact, ready to attribute much, though not all, of the difference between civilized and uncivilized peoples to racial capacities.[6] His contemporary, Theodor Waitz, took a clearer stand. Darwin attributed civilization to biological traits produced by natural selection and implied that present moral and intellectual differences among peoples are results of diverse operations of natural selection in various environments. It is instructive to compare that view with the one presented by Waitz, in a work produced just one year before *The Origin of Species* was published.[7] The two men represent totally different interpretations of cultural diversity, a distinction maintained among many humanists and biologists today. Since Waitz was self-consciously trying to ennunciate an historical perspective that has since been more widely accepted but seldom stated so clearly, his presentation can help define some of the important issues in current discussion on this topic.

Waitz was reacting to a current argument that there are biological differences in capacity for civilization and that progress is a product of a superior innate endowment.[8] This was not chiefly a moral issue for him. The race problem had been discussed in America as a "party question," but as he saw it the matter had become a subject of unprejudiced, serious study in England since the emancipation of Negroes.[9] He meant to keep it at that level.

He also responded, with an unusual awareness of his intellectual heritage, to principal tenets of the idea of progress. The basic point that civilization cannot be understood as a product of human nature pervades Waitz's work. Change, he insisted, is not natural or normal or inevitable. There is no quality in men generally, or in some peoples particularly, that moves them to civilization. Instead, an inertia or lethargy mark most people most of the time. Hume was right: There is no general desire for intellectual progress. So, while advancement of knowledge is a principal cause of civilization, knowledge does not originate of itself, nor is it a product merely of time (or of hypertrophy). Knowledge is not some magical emanation of mind; it is, rather, "nourished and matured by the historical events" which befall people.[10] Waitz's recognition of the fact of change together with his refusal to accept change as natural led him to account for change historically, and thus to explain cultural differences.

As a wide-ranging anthropologist, Waitz was prepared to see civilization as a product of several connected causes. Man's physical organization and the psychological life peculiar to each people are the dimensions chiefly considered by him. He attended also to the different physical environments in which peoples have found themselves.

Waitz regarded the physical differences among peoples as dependent on changes in conditions of life. The evidence for extensive changes *within* a human population over time suggested to him that present differences *among* peoples could have been produced by changes, and this argued for the unity of the human race. Such evidence did not appeal to him as supporting unity of descent among varieties of men, however: the differences between Negro and European might be no greater than known differences displayed by a single people over time, but that does not imply that Europeans descended from Negroes, or the reverse. On both of these questions Waitz was tentative, respectful of the evidence, sensitive to its limitations at the time.[11]

It is when Waitz comes to the psychological part of his investigation that the real point of his analysis appears. If we want to find out why one people becomes civilized while another people remains in a primitive state, we have, Waitz observed, a most difficult question on our hands. There has been "an inclination to cut the matter short, by assuming a different endowment for individual races,—an assumption rendered probable by the description of the chief features of the thoughtless Negro, the restless nomadic American, the cannibal south-islander." To ascribe the various states of civilization in which men are found to different psychic qualities is to stop inquiry into historical causes of those various states, "thus leaving the various phenomena of progressive civilization unexplained."[12] Waitz was not saying that the capacities of peoples had nothing to do with the presence or absence of civilized activities among them. Rather, he was pursuing the plain argument that an attribution of civilizing qualities to a civilized people did not explain their civilization any more than endowing nomads with nomadic qualities explained their nomadism.

The specific question that must be answered, according to Waitz, is the one that Darwin abandoned: What is it that occasions one people to change its ways so that it takes a course to a condition called civilization, while nothing of the sort had happened to that people before and is not happening to most other peoples at the time? That is, why do these differences exist in the conditions of a given people from time to time and in the conditions of distinct peoples at a given time?

Waitz paid close attention to geographical factors as possible determinants and acknowledged their great importance. He believed, however, that Montesquieu had exaggerated their influence inasmuch as they could not be made to account for the move out of a primitive state. Features such as climate and resources can shape a people's mode of life and affect the subsistence available, but these factors, Waitz argued, have a positive or negative effect on a people's move out of the primitive state only insofar as they have consequences in new activities. This is most evident, he thought, in the migrations of peoples and in their wars. These may be considered results of material conditions of population density, geographical location, terrain, resources, and so forth. But migration and war become "potent levers acting on civilization" only by virtue of the challenge presented to people by the demands of a new land and the organizational requirements of military activity. Or, again, while human migration is a response to physical conditions, it is the consequent mixing of peoples that provides the stimulus to civilization, as opposed to the fixity imposed by isolation. This mixing is primarily a matter of customs and habits of thought and action, but Waitz recognized the possibility of productive physical mixing, though he felt, again, that effects of the latter are very difficult to ascertain.[13]

For Waitz, then, anthropology takes its essential character from its concern with "differences in the various forms of human life." He saw historians as describers of the experience of civilized societies, but anthropologists are put in a position of having a *problem* on their hands as soon as they observe within the range of their attention—within man everywhere—a great diversity of life activities. When Waitz accepted diversity as a problem, his inquiries took on qualities that stand in sharp contrast to those of developmentalists in his own and following days. Now the argument that "higher" races must replace "lower" ones is revealed for what it is: a skirting of the problem of differences and a handy excuse, as Waitz put it, for exterminating the red man.[14] Now the search for a "history of civilization" or a "natural history of human society" gives way to a specification of the conditions under which old ways of life are changed into ways that we call civilized. No longer is it possible—nor does it make sense—to reduce the variety of human life activity to representations of stages in the development or evolution of a hypostatized Society or Culture or Civilization paraded under European colors. Philosophy of history and theoretical models yield to the "great variety and manifold concatenation of the conditions on which the civilization of nations depends," but within that variety kinds of circumstances are detected, and limited generalizations are offered for testing.[15] Eighteenth-century uniformitarianism gives way to the classification of different life activities by comparative historical investigation.

The moral consequences of this shift of perspective are highlighted in Theodor Waitz's firm refusal to accept European civilization as the end or goal of all historical process. He thought it methodologically correct to proceed on an assumption that the human race is one and human nature everywhere the same, but it did not follow that a uniform civilization would once prevail over the entire world. Certainly he hoped that peoples might come to a knowledge of themselves and of their social lives that would promote a moral community including all. But the variety of conditions and circumstances in which peoples live cannot, he observed, be encompassed by a single civilization. If there is to be a future universal community, surely different peoples will play different parts in it, and that arrangement will rest on a variety of summed experiences, not on a variety of biological types. Clearly, Waitz concluded, European civilization does not qualify as such a community, or as the basis for it. European civilization, he acknowledged sadly, is of questionable value to all peoples; but the important point is that any civilization pressed on others can destroy them.[16]

Waitz's type of historical anthropology, with its rejection of developmentalism, unilinear schemes of evolution, and biological explanations of differences, did not prevail in the second half of the nineteenth century, but it had illustrious representation. The German school of comparative and historical jurisprudence marched a similar route in its recognition of diversity and in its devotion to historical empiricism. In Britain, Henry Sumner Maine simply could not take seriously an attribution of differences in legal institutions to biological characters, and he was deeply puzzled by developmentalists who presumed to depict histories of institutions by tearing different institutional forms out of context and juggling them into an imagined time series. In comparing the legal histories of a group of related Indo-European peoples, Maine's objective was to discover and account for the differences in their experiences with a common set of problems, not to construct a generalized history of Aryan law, much less a treatise on the evolution of law. Austinian and utilitarian propositions about universal attributes of human nature were of no use to him in that endeavor, and he set them aside as tedious and misleading. It was in the histories of Hindu and Celt, Slav and Roman, that a real explanation of their law was to be sought.[17] His fellow jurist, Frederic William Maitland, summed it up at the beginning of the twentieth century by observing that anthropology had "the choice between being history or nothing."[18]

As anthropologists and sociologists have struggled to free their disciplines from the stultifying effects of explaining differences biologically, more has been achieved in refuting the claims of racial theorists than in finding an alternative explanation. The tasks of describing the nature of culture and society, of analyzing their constituent parts or aspects, and of relating those parts or aspects structurally and functionally have occupied the major attention of social scientists in this century. Where differences have been noticed they have usually been taken for granted, as something to be expected, given the vicissitudes of history. Thus when Franz Boas argued that the minds of primitive men as we find them today are in no way inferior to the minds of the ancestors of races who are now the most highly civilized, and that we cannot therefore account for different degrees of civilization by different racial aptitudes, he offered no real alternative reason for the differences, beyond the classical developmentalist thesis. He said the differences were of degree and were a product simply of time—some peoples have developed more rapidly than others, and this has been a result of chance or accident. Boas was certainly not ruling out the possibility of saying something significant about the historical events that facilitated civilization, but his chief purpose, in this context, was to demonstrate the inadequacies of a racial explanation of civilization.[19]

A more positive and systematic statement of the problem of cultural differences, and of a historical theory of differences, has been offered in this century by Frederick J. Teggart.[20] Teggart's point of departure was a rejection of racial or biological and of physical environmental interpretations of differences. His interest in differences centered on what he called backward and advanced cultures, or uncivilized and civilized peoples, rather than on the minutiae of cultural variety. In his anxiety to avoid the banalities of the idea of progress, he found it difficult to identify these social and cultural types. What he spoke of actually, however, is what can be called active and inactive peoples. The central question for him is the persistent one in this tradition: What gets a people on the move out of longstanding ways of thought and action? How does Walter Bagehot's "cake of custom" get broken? What releases or forces peoples, and individuals, from old social and cultural confines?

Teggart claimed no originality for his answers to these questions, but his theory did bring together hitherto unconnected strands of thought. Starting from the observation that people have exhibited no inherent drive or propensity to improve or change their way of life, he noted that most peoples had in fact made no significant changes in their social arrangements or cultural activities, so far as the dated historical record went. Gradual modifications of existing conditions had occurred; extensions and intensifications of traditional forms were com-

mon. But by and large Teggart agreed with Hume (and
with Darwin for that matter) that fixity and persistence
are the prevailing processes in the histories of men. Civilizations as processes or accomplishments stand in glar-
ing contrast to this scene of relative inactivity. Civilization must be seen, Teggart insisted, as a rare and
scattered phenomenon.

When a kind of human historical activity is plotted in
time and space and revealed to be sporadic, its distribution calls for explanation. Inasmuch as it stands in contrast to other forms of such activity, the problem posed is
that of cultural and social differences. Reference to a
common humanity or common human nature, Teggart
pointed out, is of no help in solving the problem. Reference to different human natures that are supposed to
derive either from distinct original races or from direct or
indirect action of diverse environments has so far, he
noted, yielded no supportable answers. This situation
requires a determination of time and place circumstances
under which a given people changes its basic life pattern, compared with and distinguished from the time
and place circumstances under which another given people retains and continues a traditional life pattern. The
same problem and the same requirements are posed, of
course, when attention is shifted to the different circumstances of the same people before and after its move from
an old to a changed way of life. Teggart was saying that
cultural differences must be explained by the historical
and geographical conditions under which peoples have
led their lives.

Because civilization is a rare and spotty thing, because,
more generally speaking, peoples have only occasionally
abandoned customary and hitherto satisfying activities,

Teggart concluded that profound and pervasive alterations of living conditions are required to overcome a prevalent cultural torpor. The clues he picked up at this point are similar to those we have noted in the eighteenth- and nineteenth-century literature. Peoples' lives have been disrupted, he agreed, by migrations and accompanying conflicts. Teggart was shaping these ideas at a time when historical geographers were engaged in exciting discoveries and speculations about migrations in the Eurasian land mass associated with drastic climatic changes. This was the kind of disrupting event that he saw as capable of driving a people from its homeland, bringing it into conflict with encountered peoples, forcing it to solve novel problems of subsistence, and requiring new social organizations of work and military activities.

In broader perspective, Teggart saw the great cultural efflorescences—Hugh Murray's "classic ages"—as products of peoples' confrontations with a breakdown of old institutional and cultural arrangements in the face of new demands occasioned by a serious threat to their subsistence as a population and existence as a social or political unit. He also regarded a people's exposure to an alien and contradictory idea system as similarly disruptive, and so conducive to innovative thought. In any case, the sort of change Teggart envisaged as civilization-producing is sudden, rapid, and permeative. It stands in contrast to processes of persistence depicted in functional theory and to processes of slow, gradual, and continuous change portrayed in developmentalist or evolutionist theory. Civilizational change is presented as *eventful*. Change occurs in this case because something *happens*. Inquiry is directed, therefore, to a determination of classes of events that bring about changes resulting in the array of cultural differences observable in the present.

Because he regarded historical changes as the work of individuals, Teggart thought that an explanation of a thing like civilization must describe the ways in which persons come to think and act differently from one time to another. He spoke, therefore, of the shattering events associated with migration and conflict "releasing" individuals from the bondage of custom and casting them into situations where they are without old solutions to problems of action and old ideal orientations to problems of faith and intellect. It is under such conditions that creativity in both thought and action can occur.

The American sociologist Robert E. Park took this facet of Teggart's formulation and developed it into a concept of the "marginal man."[21] Park's object, also, was to explain existing cultural differences among peoples, and he was convinced that racial and physical environmental theories have failed to do so. He agreed that migrations and the collisions incident to them have been potent causes of civilization, but he chose to focus on the individual in that context and to attend particularly to the process of disruption as it occurred in the movements and migrations of peoples in cities during the expansion of Europe. "In these great cities," he said, "where all the passions, all the energies of mankind are released, we are in a position to investigate the processes of civilization, as it were, under a microscope." Park detected in the "meetings and minglings" of people in cities a turmoil that catches certain groups of people on the "margin" between two cultures. His prime example is the Jew, who, once he leaves the ghetto and is allowed to take part in the life of the people surrounding him, is confronted in acute form with the dilemmas that Teggart saw besetting the migrant in Eurasia—he is cut off from old supports, facing new problems, and exposed to alien customs and modes of thought. He is caught between a traditional orientation to life which he must leave and a new one of which he is not wholly trustful and into which he is not truly admitted. Thus, "It is in the mind of the marginal man—where the changes and fusions of culture are going on—that we can best study the processes of civilization and of progress." It is in the reactions of marginal man that creativity may be observed.

Although in one sense he tried to look more closely at the particulars of what Teggart described broadly, Park also sought to extend the scope of what he regarded as the "catastrophic" theory of civilization. Migrations and subsequent clashes of whole peoples could be regarded as only a part, though an important part, of a class of commotions and dislocations experienced by human societies. Revolutions, enlightenments, religious crusades, wars, and other disruptive occurrences have also been occasions for decomposing old orders and providing the circumstances in which individuals act to bring about historic changes.

Where Park looked through a microscope at the challenges faced by people in situations of cultural stress and disorder, A. J. Toynbee [22] took the whole array of civilizational histories as a field of inquiry. His starting point was the astonishing range of existing cultural differences in the world. As he saw it, these differences were the product of only the last five or six thousand years of human history. Although men had reached substantially their present biological status hundreds of thousands of

139

years ago, they had only recently and on rare occasions (Toynbee counted twenty-one) formed societies of the type we call civilizations. In almost all instances, human societies had not made this particular move and remained on a "primitive" level. How, Toynbee asked, is the difference to be accounted for?

Like his predecessors in this kind of investigation, Toynbee looked first to the biological answer. But he could find no evidence of a correlation of biological and cultural differences. Nor was the physical environmental theory of much help: areas in which civilizations have arisen are paralleled by similar areas in which they have not. In these circumstances Toynbee turned to what had happened in the places and times of civilization. Happenings did not present themselves in the record in anything other than temporal and spatial patterns, of course, so Toynbee had to approach the record with an idea, a hypothesis, a guess. He chose, in broad terms, the thesis developed in the work of his predecessors Hume and Waitz and Teggart.

Toynbee, however, had a style, often displayed by humanist scholars, that causes some misunderstanding by natural scientists. He commonly described his venture in historical research as an exploration of the mystery of the universe, and he frankly confessed that he looked to mythology for leads and key ideas. His basic proposition that civilizations result from the successful responses of peoples to particular challenges they encounter in their historical experience was paraded by him as an insight derived from Goethe's *Faust*, a perspective in harmony with the theme of the universal drama in which God accepts Mephistopheles' challenge to destroy His fairest work. The idea, nevertheless, is substantially one with the "catastrophic" theory, and, as Dobzhansky remarked, its imagery can even be used to epitomize the interactive relationship between the environment and the organism, as it is represented in Darwinian theory.[23] In any event, Toynbee took cultural differences as a central humanist problem and one that must be attacked on the level of social and cultural histories, not evolutionary biology.

Acceptance of the problem of differences and search for solutions in historical rather than genetic terms have recently been represented effectively in the work of Alexander Alland, Jr.[24] Taking differences as anthropology's proper concern, Alland urges a historical, rather than a biological, explanation of them on the ground that the former is simpler and covers the known facts. He stresses the importance of contact between peoples as a stimulant to creative thinking. It is in an exchange of ideas, as he puts it, not in an exchange of genes, that old frameworks of thought are transcended and fresh viewpoints shaped. The accomplishments of Greek philosophers and scientists, of Elizabethan writers, of Flemish painters, or of German musicians are understandable, he argues, not in terms of biological changes that occurred antecedent to their periods of intense activity, but in the light of peculiar conjunctions of outlooks and juxtapositions of contrasting world views. These are the conditions under which changes have taken place because something happened, and, therefore, the conditions under which differentiation has occurred.

Apart from their merit, these examples of historical accountings for cultural diversity can be seen to involve a kind of explanation that is quite different from those of-

141

fered either by classical social or cultural evolutionists or by biologists.

Insofar as both of the latter groups have tended to stress cultural similarities or uniformities and to relegate diversity to a category of the accidental or superficial, the problem of differences is not even raised. The quest for continuity in nature—in both a chain of being and in a gradual process of becoming or change—can be so consuming as to lead to a designation of any concern with diversity as preoccupation with the supernatural or as dabbling in exotic frills. It is most unfortunate that this feature of nineteenth-century social evolutionism has found renewed expression in twentieth-century sociobiology. It should be apparent that the concern of a Hume or a Waitz or a Teggart was not with inconsequential variations on basically similar themes. They were aware of the most profound differences in human life patterns that the historical and archaeological and ethnographic records display, and, with a view to enhancing rational control over human life activities, they sought an understanding of events and conditions that had produced the various known forms of those activities.

Insofar as those who seek biological explanations of human social and cultural life extend that form of inquiry to social and cultural differences, their approach is distinguished from the historical by an insistence on going "behind" the world of happenings to find a producer of happenings—a "great constructor" like natural selection, or sets of inherent ideas that move peoples along different paths, or racial capacities or genotypes that manifest themselves in diverse cultural lives. The drawback of such an approach has been and is that it leaves behind the empirical historical world of human

142

experience and seeks to reconstruct experience from conceptual models. A result is that there can be no return to an actual world of experience to which theory might sensitize us, for a hypothetical world has been created and taken for real. That is what Theodor Waitz meant when he said that the postulation of human biological differences stopped historical inquiry into human social differences *ab initio*. It is what Frederick Teggart meant when he said that in the study of history the laboratory must give place to the world.

The reconstruction of human history by such biologists as Edward O. Wilson and Konrad Lorenz is accomplished almost entirely from conjectures about how natural selection *would have operated* to produce certain results. The speculative quality of this enterprise is indicated by the fact that informed biologists differ in their reconstructions at least as widely as humanist scholars have. Eighteenth- and nineteenth-century developmentalist or progress theorists of history proceeded in a similar manner. In their case the ordering concept was not selection but an image of a certain potential in human nature or history itself which was supposed to unfold through time, if nothing interfered. The process depicted was therefore orthogenetic and teleological. In both cases, however, reconstruction has proceeded with scant reference to historical records of times when and places where events in human experience occurred.

If sociobiology is to gain adherents among social scientists, the theory must be used in the actual arena of human histories. A demonstration of the operation of natural selection in concrete historical settings is needed. Was this process involved in the disintegration of the Roman Empire? Was it effective in producing the industrial revolution in Western Europe, or the Elizabethan literary era? Did natural selection work to instigate or guide the Protestant Reformation? Was it operative (as Darwin suggested vaguely) in the European imperial venture? What is wanted here, of course, is evidence of actual natural selection and not the tired suggestion that the most effective ideas or institutions tend to prevail in the long run. And then the way in which changes in gene pools affect social and cultural activities must be specified.[25]

When human activity is described merely as a consequence of genetic predispositions in human nature produced by natural selection, the most that has been accomplished—granting the accuracy of the statement—is the naming or definition of the activity. When we go on to categorize all these predispositions as aspects of a basic drive to improve the inclusive fitness of actors, the explanation further loses significance as historical accounting. To say that Napoleon, on June 14, 1800, in the battle of Marengo, was acting to improve his inclusive fitness, and that Michelangelo, when he undertook the Sistine Chapel painting in 1508, was acting to improve his inclusive fitness, is to shed very little light on those actions, even if the statements were true. Explanation by "ultimate" causes is intriguing, but these can be so remote as to be pointless. Such propositions make small contribution to our understanding of the part played by the Napoleonic wars in shaping the structure of modern Europe or of the effective circumstances and conditions of the Italian Renaissance. As François Jacob has pointed out, concepts or generalizations that are explanatory at one level of complexity may still hold true at another level but are trivial so far as a comprehension of the additional complications of the situation is concerned. This

144

is particularly the case where conceptions of physical and organic phenomena underlying a historical situation fail to comprehend the historical circumstances as such.[26] When Caesar crossed the Rubicon on January 10, 49 B.C., that motion in space had to be made against friction, and Caesar's behavior might well have been aggressive and prompted by a genetic disposition to enhance his inclusive fitness, but that analysis of the behavior fails to grasp it as a signal of the fall of the Roman republic and portent of the rise of an empire that would shape the lives of European populations for centuries to come. A physical and biological description and explanation of Caesar's behavior on that occasion would hardly touch on the historical import of his act.

The inclination to regard the activities of a Napoleon, a Michelangelo, or a Caesar as the proximate, not the ultimate, factors in history, draws attention away from the empirical context in which theories of human history must be used and tested. Occupation with such historical detail does not mean commitment to a doctrine of free will and a search for explanation in the random motives of individuals. It does mean that the would-be explainer has before him at all times the concrete world of observed events and not a set of hypothetical occurrences deduced from conceptual models. The difference for inquiry is crucial. Attempts to account historically for social and cultural differences result from an acceptance of a plurality of histories as the ultimate data of human experience, and from a refusal to postulate entities or forces that produce a make-believe history.

When we ask what biologists might contribute to an explanation of cultural differences, the first and most obvious answer is that they might identify human biological types that correlate with cultural types. Biologists have failed however, both to clearly identify biological types, and, especially, to demonstrate how the organic traits used to describe the types operate to produce cultural traits. Until both of these tasks are in hand, such explanations of cultural differences remain at the tautological level of postulating a biological propensity for any given social or cultural phenomenon. Except for a continuing and apparently unsuccessful effort to fix upon genetically based population differences in intelligence, with the implication that this would determine varying capacities for designated cultural activities, biologists have in recent years largely abandoned this approach to the problem.

It is now suggested, instead, that cultural differences are to be understood as various adaptations to various environments. Human geographers have, of course, long explored that thesis in describing ways of life that are adjustments to different circumstances of subsistence and survival, adjustments that constitute part of the social arrangements and cultural elements that are the traditions of peoples. Whether the functions of such traditions have in any way or to any extent been performed by biological mechanisms produced by natural selection in a process of social or cultural adaptation in a strict Darwinian sense is quite another matter. To ask "whether an infant Nilotic Negro could in fact become a 'complete' representative of Eskimo culture"[27] is legitimate, and if population geneticists could shed light on it that would be a light social scientists would be foolish to ignore. To the extent that there is any such light, it is still, apparently, in the form of theory, but the possibility of selection for

146

different genotypic characteristics favored by different environments and having significant effects on social and cultural activities cannot be denied out of hand. However, biologists should be forewarned that they are dealing here with actual histories where conclusions must be tested against recorded experiences, not working theories.

The absence to date of hard evidence for historical processes of social adaptation leaves social scientists with the alternative of seeking explanations of social and cultural differences in other historical terms. Biologists have their own road to travel in this matter, a hard road, apparently, strewn with enormous technical problems. Social scientists cannot be obliged to walk that road; it is evidently a waste of time even for biologists in other specialties. The "cooperation" of social scientists in the sociobiological venture is not likely to be of much help to sociobiologists, and is more likely to produce the barren, or worse, consequences of prior humanist rides on biological bandwagons.

There is a class of biological phenomena that could be of great interest to social scientists and about which an interchange of ideas might take place. This has to do with opportunistic activities, or different forms of adjustment (as distinguished from adaptation) to environments, within animal species other than man. The reference here is not to those isolated items of so-called culture in animals that are sometimes cited for the purpose of demonstrating continuity in nature or the oneness of human beings with other organisms. Rather, it appears to be the case that some species of animals, vertebrates most probably, react to changes in the environment with actions that are not to be regarded as ge-

147

netically guided in the direct fashion true of their ordinary behavior. Variations other than seasonal in food supply, the appearance of a new type of food or predator, radical and sudden changes in terrain or other aspects of habitat, and many other alterations of environment that result from human intrusion, give rise from time to time and from place to place to activities in one population of a species that were not there before and are not present among other populations of the species. Such activities are often significant to the extent that they are directly related to individual survival, and they can arise and disappear with a speed that rules out genetic change as explanation.

Do animal populations have "histories" in this sense?[28] This might seem to be the case if their activities change as a result of something happening that does not have its effect simply through the pressure of natural selection on phenotypic variations. How such happenings do come to have their effects on the actions of animals would be of great interest to students of man, especially if explanation goes beyond a negative observation of genetic underprescription or behavioral flexibility to a linkage of kinds of experiences with kinds of innovative activities. A discussion of such phenomena might, at least, lead to a clearer perception and deeper appreciation of the significance of historical phenomena among humans as compared with other animals.

CHAPTER **6**

HUMAN NATURE
AND CULTURE

A basic disagreement between biologists and humanists arises from a misunderstanding of the concepts of human society and human culture.[1] The result is that biologists talk about a coral society or beaver society or baboon society as if these were of a kind with human society and all could therefore be taken as the proper subject matter of a general social science. This misconception is then compounded by the assumption that nonhuman societies (and, to some degree, human hunter-gatherer societies) display most clearly the ultimate biological sources of all society, and by the conclusion that social science, as a branch of biology, must therefore concentrate on those elementary forms of social life.

Social theorists have done much to encourage this view. They likened people to other animals centuries before the biological sciences achieved their modern form, and they drew analogies between human societies and animal societies before biologists took the comparison seriously. The long-entrenched use of organic concepts of all sorts in the human sciences has, in a pervasive manner, prepared a ground in general thinking for the claim that human social facts are really biological facts. No doubt some biologists find support for such a proposition when they observe that many of the basic concepts of social science are couched in biological terms, even though the concepts originated in social theory and were borrowed by biology.

The humanistic disciplines have complicated this situation by sometimes seeming to describe society and culture as "things" that have certain qualities capable of producing certain results. In their eagerness to call attention to the independence of sociocultural phenomena, sociologists and anthropologists have thus appeared to establish a sort of ontology of society and culture. This is regarded by critics as reification, which involves a departure from empiricism. What humanists call biological reductionism can be presented as an attempt to avoid the attribution of vague powers to shadowy objects and to get down to the basic elements of social behavior. Sociobiologists might claim that they are thus trying to call social scientists to empirical account.

It seems unlikely that the argument over reification and reductionism, and the tendency to carry it to metaphysical questions of ultimate causation, can be pursued with profit. My objective in this chapter is, instead, to suggest that efforts to account historically for social and cultural differences reveal aspects of human societies and cultures that cannot be derived from human nature as a unity or from hypostatized Society and Culture. Human society and culture are real only as kinds of societies and cultures, and kinds of human societies and

cultures are evident and understandable only as historical products, not as biological products.

We can compare the histories of cultures only if we are
aware that cultures exist. Cultural differences can have
no significance for those who do not recognize cultures.
Cultural differences in that case appear as facts attendant
on other things that cause them and are consequently
more real and basic. Diversity is seen as variation around
a type and, therefore, as troublesome interference with a
clear vision of what the type really is. Lack of concern
about cultural differences and emphasis on cultural universals are rooted in denial of the existence of human
culture as it is conceived by most anthropologists.

When we read early descriptions of human groups it is
often with a sense that the writer had no definite plan of
observation. There is vagrant movement from one topic
to another, and especially between descriptions of the
appearance of persons and accounts of their doings.
Much of even the classical Greek and Roman historical
literature is of this kind. Marco Polo's narrative, rich
though it be, is flawed by such shapelessness. Most of
the accounts of European voyage and discovery exasper-
ate a reader who seeks to compare in broad terms Carib
and Tahitian, Iroquois and Aztec. This is because the
writers worked with no clear image of what constituted
an aggregation of persons as a unit distinct from other
aggregations; hence the common practice of attending to
personal appearance, including dress and adornment, as
a clue to identity.

It is only recently that observers of the human scene
have come to grips with their subject matter by system-

atic refinement of concepts of society and culture. The process has been long and difficult, and present results are far from satisfactory, but it will be a serious misfortune if the individualistic orientation of biological evolution theory is used to revive that atomistic view of human groups that so long obscured the effects of association, interaction, tradition, and common historical experiences in human life.

In the history of European thought, an explicit recognition of sociocultural units as such, and their differentiation, is first clear in the Renaissance. Europeans became aware then that the state of artistic, literary, philosophic, and scientific activities among themselves differed greatly from what they had come to know about such activities in classical antiquity. A conscious comparison was drawn between past and present, and for that purpose some kind of identification of comparable units had to be made.[2] As Europeans came later to contemplate the great panorama of alien peoples exposed to them by voyages of discovery, commerce, proselytism, and colonization, this consciousness of differences was sharpened and, in keeping with the idea of progress, the differences were defined as degrees of development in a universal process leading to a European kind of society and culture. Despite the ethnocentric denial of basic differences in this attitude, the notion that *something* was developing was clearly implied. Definition of the something, and of its parts—law, family, religion, art—was a major task early anthropologists and sociologists set themselves.[3]

Now if we look again at the men discussed in the last chapter, it might appear that their efforts to formulate historical explanations of differences depended upon an answer to the question: differences in *what?* Given the nonformalist character of their thinking, however, they were not inclined to regard diversity as a characteristic of some entity that produced, or was the ultimate source of, human experiences. Biological and physical environmental explanations of differences were rejected in favor of historical explanations, and this involved them in the difficult task of *identifying social and cultural phenomena as results of historical processes.* Different kinds of social or cultural results were to be explained by different kinds of historical experiences.

David Hume obviously struggled with this problem. Animals other than man owe their nature, he acknowledged, to air, food, and climate, but the case of human beings is "curious" by virtue of the experience of entering "deeply into each other's sentiments." Today we refer to this as a social process; Hume called it a "moral" cause to distinguish it from physical and biological causes of national character. Nations, as Hume saw it, take on their distinguishing characteristics in this process; the process itself is efficient; the interactions are productive of national characters.

Hume could not regard this moral cause simply as a constant determinant of a uniform result. That was impossible because his object was to explain particular differences among peoples. He wanted to account for actual variation in the activities of people, not for Society or Culture. He sought to do this by tracing diversity to the various forms and historical circumstances of interactions among persons. For the differences that interested Hume, interactions among persons in situations of disruption of traditional behavior were of central importance. What sociologists today call the social factor took on reality for Hume only in specified kinds of historical situations.[4]

In the case of James Dunbar the emphasis was, again, on intercourse among people and the circumstances of that intercourse. Interchanges shape persons and peoples, he pointed out, but interaction was not to be regarded as a uniform process producing like results. It had historical dimensions that led to different results. Dunbar was particularly impressed with the civilizing effects of contact between civilized and uncivilized peoples, but in general he was saying that any given human condition is to be seen as a result of mutual influences among human beings in a variety of settings. Different patterns of events lead to different results from the same kind of social processes.[5]

With Hugh Murray, the focus of attention was on communication among persons and groups of persons, a process of interaction that had different consequences depending on the degree of freedom in which it was carried on—freedom in the sense of an absence of barriers among individuals as well as in the sense of a relaxation or removal of customary and habitual modes of thought and action. These conditions of freedom, for Murray, are historical conditions that in themselves shape the results of interactions and exchanges in human relations and have their substance in the acts of persons in certain situations rather than in timeless and universal qualities of Society or Culture.[6]

Search for the social or cultural in history is especially evident in Theodor Waitz's anthropology. While he elaborated no concept of society or of culture and worked only with such conventional concepts as knowledge or mind or civilization, it is nevertheless plain that his acceptance of the problem of differences led him at once to recognize that postulation of variety in racial endowment or in physical environment as the cause of the differences meant ignoring something of great and immediate importance. So, while such factors as climate and material resources obviously must be acknowledged as important influences on modes of life, their effects are mediated by their "social" consequences—that is, the new collective activities demanded by changed physical circumstances, or the stimulating exchange of ideas and modes of action following a mixing of peoples through migrations forced by material conditions. The potency of these social factors, together with the enormous range of civilizational achievement, led Waitz to conclude that the limited racial diversity observable cannot account for the various accomplishments of peoples, even if the way in which those biological differences manifested themselves in cultural activities were understood.

In his discussion of mind and knowledge, Waitz again saw clearly that he was dealing with sociocultural phenomena. Knowledge results from activities of persons in concert with one another—from *social* activity—from "the combined activity of all individuals living together." And the persons in any given case are products of particular surroundings and of their historical experiences, their concerted activities in the broadest sense. For Waitz social relations in the sense of interactions among individuals and among groups constitute the stuff of history in which answers to the problem of differences are to be sought. One group of causes of civilization must be looked for in "the sum total of social relations and connexions of individuals and circles of society, internally and externally." But these were not abstract traits of an abstract society, for Waitz; they took their rise and shape from the historical activities of people under quite particular conditions.[7]

Investigators like Teggart, Park, and Toynbee made it clear that when they spoke of human histories, whether in broad or narrow compass, they referred to human activities in which people created social structures and cultural forms and in so doing shaped themselves. The marginal man, the innovator, and the responder to challenges are not biological types produced by natural selection or any other organic process. Nor are they social or cultural types produced by universal processes or by a dynamic in human nature. Adam Ferguson was mistaken in saying that men would always be improving their ways. Persons who act to bring about sociocultural changes appear typically under certain historical circumstances of stress and disruption of habitual modes of action, and they act as they do because they have had the experience of that kind of milieu. Tradition-bound, conventional, and inactive men are similarly results of circumstances that have tended to the preservation of customary thought and action, circumstances that assure satisfactory consequences from old ways of doing things, circumstances that are served by prevailing conduct, rather than conditions that demand solutions to new problems.

It is because they were interested in both persistence and change in kinds of human activities that thinkers of this school were face to face with the problem of differences and could not explain diversity in terms of universal human nature. Because the change in activities they observed was sporadic in time and place, and often rapid, it could not be understood as a function of a slow and continuous evolutionary process. Because the processes of change and persistence did not correlate with typical geographical settings they could not be accounted for in physical environmental terms. Because there was no evidence of a match between identifiable biological types and active or inactive peoples, that explanation had to be put aside. It was in these circumstances of facing the problem of differences among peoples, and of eliminating one by one possible solutions, that investigators arrived at the position of identifying a *kind* of happening, event, condition, or circumstance that is *sui generis*—the human social and cultural kind. Social and cultural differences are explained as results of historical experiences, and because the social and cultural are real only in their particular forms, the attempt to identify and analyze society and culture must proceed with a comparison of histories.

People are seen as products of experience. Experience always occurs in physical settings, and human experience is always something that implies the presence of human organisms. But different experiences have different results for groups of similar human organisms in similar physical settings. The differences consist in the kinds of human relationships and interactions and in the effects of these interactions.

It can be useful now to return to a point raised in the discussion of comparisons of man and other animals.

Many kinds of animals live in societies in the sense of individuals existing in close active relationship, interacting in ways that are significant for ontogeny, learning to some extent by tradition, cooperating or competing in common activities, and behaving generally with an awareness of or interest in others. If we ask how human societies differ from these other animal societies we can answer that in all the respects mentioned human societies manifest such traits in far greater degree of intensity, scope, and effect, and that this is a consequence of qualities in human beings—most notably, symbol-making and symbol-using power—that other animals do not possess in anything like the same degree.

A related approach to the question is suggested by the observation that humans are the only animals that have histories. All species are products of the evolutionary time process. But, for given periods of historical time, *Homo sapiens* differs radically from other social species in the degree to which his social life changes with no apparent reference to evolutionary changes, and in the varieties of sociocultural life that are simultaneously displayed within the species.[8] These enormous changes and striking differences are not results of biological or physical changes. They are results of historical human activities. To say, then, that human beings have histories is to say they have societies and cultures in a sense that other animals do not.

In this context, historical change means change brought about by the activities of people in association with one another. It is cultural and social change in that sense. What is changed is the kind and product of human activities and the form of association in which the activities are carried on. It is cultural and social change in that sense, too. This is the significance of the observation that man makes his own history, and in so doing, makes himself, as a social actor and a cultural creator and carrier. People do not just "have" histories in the sense that animals may be said to have had evolutionary pasts or to have had things happen to them. People make history by their social actions, and they are conscious of history as something of their own making. As George Cornewall Lewis observed, man is "something more than a mere gregarious animal."[9]

This idea that human beings can actually bring something of significance into existence by their own social and cultural activities has been difficult to grasp. The dialogue between humanists and biologists could be more productive if the idea were more clearly understood. First, it is necessary to dissociate the proposition from crude notions about free will bringing things to pass contrary to nature and to the axiom, *nihil ex nihilo*. The problem of free will has long been of concern to social theorists and, we have noticed, it continues to plague even sociobiologists. But the problem of how people might reach decisions to act that are not understandable as direct results of either organic dispositions or discernible social and cultural experience must be distinguished from the question of how activity in itself has consequences for social structure and cultural content. What people thought and did in the Protestant Reformation shaped that series of events and produced changes in the economic activities and class structure of European societies. Why they thought and acted so is a legitimate question, which can be pursued in antecedent history as well as in terms of biological drives and constraints. The matter of free will can be disregarded in both these lines of inquiry. Social scientists would claim, with strong evidence, that their explanations have been better in such instances than those offered by biologists. But setting that question aside, there is no prima facie reason to regard explanation couched in terms of social activities as any less real or natural than explanation from genetic disposition. There is no warrant for assuming that assignment of biological causes to human activities is more materialistic than a specification of historical causes. People act and their actions have consequences. There is nothing mystical or tentative or proximate about that observation.

The impression that there is something mysterious about the effectiveness of human activity in itself results, apparently, from a common belief that what happens in time must be understood either as accident or as a result of the operation of a substantial thing—a natural entity. Thus George Gaylord Simpson has said that "changeless immanent forces" must be the source of history and that Darwin's understanding of the sequences of historical events resulting in organic systems came from a discovery of processes that are "inherent in the nature of the cosmos."[10] Human history, by such a line of reasoning, is also conceived as a product of immanent forces, forces that reside in human nature, considered as an object.

Whatever may be the service of this idea in the natural sciences, it should be recognized as a particular intellectual orientation to the world, not an obvious truth. It is also an idea that has been exploited time and again by humanists and others in futile efforts to find the cause and meaning of human history. It was this notion that dominated the human sciences before the reality, integrity, and independence of social and cultural activity came to be accepted. It is this belief that has led to a search for such entities as a "geist," "culture soul," "destiny," "divine spirit," "elementary idea," or "racial genius" lying behind and giving shape to history. It has repeatedly led students of human social and cultural phenomena to lose the empirical-historical referent of their propositions in flighty quest of powers that bring things to pass. It is the most primitive and simplistic mode of explanation in man's contemplation of the world about him. There should be understanding, at least, of humanists' wariness of the most recent suggestion that genes are to be regarded as the basic architects of history.

The concepts of human society and of human culture were not formulated, of course, in response to modern sociobiology. But they were responses to and standpoints against a similar brand of thought. Its eighteenth-century form is best expressed, perhaps, in Rousseau. Rousseau, it will be recalled, recognized that man differs from other animals inasmuch as he changes in the course of history. "Natural" man therefore, was quite different from the men we observe today. Another way of saying this is that human nature in the people now before us has been obscured by an overlay of features resulting from historical experience. Rousseau thought that the proper and practical study of man would undertake to remove the veneer, lay bare the genuine, original human nature, and so reveal the real basis on which social reformation must build. It would be interesting to compare this outlook with the current sociobiological view that there is now a contradiction between an old and persisting human nature and historically produced modern life conditions, a contradiction to be dealt with first of all by stripping away false notions about ourselves and coming to an understanding of what human nature really is.

The thing to be noticed, however, in both Rousseau and sociobiology, is the altogether radical idea that what has happened in human history has been a quirky mistake that now must either be undone or somehow remedied. This historical review and prospect in general outline are evident as well in some Marxist interpretations of history in which all that has happened since an early period of genuine collective life is regarded as a denial or alienation of human potential, which must now be reversed by a return to a genuine form of human social life in which new and bountiful productive forces will somehow be accommodated. And the fundamental theme of original bliss, an awful historical interim of straying from the path of righteousness, and eventual salvation in a return to innocence is, of course, the framework of the rational Christian philosophy of history epitomized in Saint Augustine.

This view that human history has somehow been a mistake because it has not been an expression of man's true nature results in a belief that the histories of peoples do not signify as experiences in varieties of social and cultural life. Human histories are seen as not in the nature of things, as fortuitous collections of events, and as accidental results of such miraculous blunders as human formation of a society and culture not in keeping with human nature.

From such a conceptual outlook history becomes unreal, and human society and culture become unreal because they are contradictions rather than manifestations of human nature. If society is to be accepted as a biological phenomenon, society must be regarded as sick; it has its only reality as a pathological phenomenon.

It is only in such a context that one can say, with Rousseau, that we must focus on man as he was in a distant past, not as we see him in the present; that we must attend to what is universal in human societies and cultures instead of to differences, because the universal is a direct expression of human nature and, therefore, real; and that what we are actually given in past histories and present cultural differences are epiphenomena of no consequence beyond their function as examples of how wrong it is to go against nature. Only from this point of view can one concur with Wilson that it is more important to know that there is everywhere a slight genetic difference between men and women than to know of the different circumstances under which various groups of women have experienced virtual slavery or virtual equality with men.

Nineteenth-century reaction against this orientation to the study of humankind was based upon a recognition of people as history-making animals whose activities have consequences that make up the actual social and cultural conditions of their lives. George Cornewall Lewis' statement of this new perspective is worth quoting at length.

Man alone, among organised beings, possesses the moral and intellectual qualities which render one generation of human beings unlike another, and which enable him to alter his own condition and that of others by self-culture. Hence he alone, of all living beings, possesses a history; other tribes of animals are described by enumerating all the properties of their species or kind, and when this task has been completely accomplished, the problem is exhausted, except so far as varieties may be produced by domestication. One generation of elephants, or monkeys, or lions, has nothing to distinguish it from another. But man, in addition to that physiological character which he has in common with other animals, and which, like their physical type, is unvarying, has also attributes which distinguish one community of men from another—and, again, one generation of the same community from another generation. It is the sum of the acts of a society, as they occur in succession, which

163

constitutes its history, and distinguishes its state, not only from that of other societies, but also from its own states, both anterior and subsequent.[11]

Waitz made essentially the same argument when he noted that something of fundamental importance goes on in human histories that cannot be derived from the aggregate of physiological and psychological facts that are *nevertheless the essential conditions of the historical facts*. This is driven home by the observation of different histories among biologically like peoples. What is going on in history, as Waitz put it, is a social process, one in which man "steps out of his individual life, and enters into a social connexion with others, by whom he himself arrives at a higher and truly human development." It is when people make this transition from isolation into social life, Waitz concluded, that "Anthropology must lay hold of man" and probe the conditions and consequences of social intercourse. Moreover, he was careful to add, we must avoid an abstract analysis of human social life as a shaper of some generalized human nature; the objective is an examination of the whole range of histories in which social processes have yielded different results.[12]

These are some of the principles by which social and cultural scientists have sought to identify their subject matter and the proper limits of their investigations. After centuries of going "behind" the social and cultural activities of people to find springs or motors to account for such phenomena, they achieved a perspective from which these facts are accepted and explanations of them are sought in their own terms. It is a serious matter when allegedly new and hitherto hidden springs are once more revealed as substitutes for the "proximate" causes found in historical "contingency." It is difficult to understand, for example, what commentators like Jacques Monod [13] seek in denying a difference between behavior determined by innate or genetic dispositions and learned behavior. When a learned behavior is a human activity present in some societies and not in others (composition and performance of polyphonic music, let us say), and we have historical information about the rise of that activity involving specific events and particular social conditions, surely that information is more helpful in understanding the presence or absence of such activity than is the observation that all human behavior is made possible by innate programs shaped by the "experience" of organic evolution. However true the latter observation, it is irrelevant to the historical question of just how the various activities of man have come to be as they are. To regard the experience of organisms in the evolutionary process as one with the experience of peoples in their social and cultural histories is to deprive the word of meaning. The search for unity in nature can be pressed too far.

Abstract statements about the ultimately innate basis of all behavior need to be brought to historical test. When that is done, their weakness becomes evident. If the objective is to define behaviors as aggressive, altruistic, territorial, etc., and then to speculate on how aggression, altruism, and territorialism might have been selected for, that is another exercise, and one that has little to do with problems of social and cultural inquiry. Hypothetical examples of the operation of natural selection cannot be substituted for human histories. Theory in the social sciences must have an empirical referent in time and place events.

In the case of the human sciences there is a unique opportunity to make this kind of empirical test, for man is not only the one animal that has histories, he is also the only animal that records his histories.[14]

In oral tradition, and especially in written documents, he reviews and interprets his experiences, and this profoundly influences the course of action. By use of symbol-making powers a people is thus able both to extend memory over a broad temporal range of history and to enrich its own experience by a knowledge of and comparison with the histories of other peoples. Just as the making and keeping of histories distinguishes human life, so the existence of historical records distinguishes social and cultural studies by providing direct evidence in the form of human testimony against which theories of history can be checked.

At this juncture in the argument an objection might be raised to the effect that products—man, his society, his culture—have been presented as if made out of nothing but disembodied acts. Whence, it could be asked, this acting man, this kind of animal, and whence the social and cultural milieu in which he finds himself? The latter part of the question, insofar as it suggests a search for origins, has not proved up to now to be a productive line of inquiry. The historical evidence of human experience always places people in social and cultural environments. Those are the concerns in which the investigator finds them. There is no reason, of course, for not following the historical evidence as far back in time as it will carry us. But conjecture and extrapolation from assumed equivalences of early human history have not contributed much to our understanding of the human condition, and they have produced a good deal of misleading nonsense. Human beings have been found only in historical contexts; explications of their conditions must rest on such contexts, as given.

The other part of the question directs us again to the problem of human nature. Is there not something about man, some humanness, that, quite apart from experiences peculiar to certain groups of men, directs his activities along channels that are different from the action paths of beavers and baboons, of woodpeckers and termites? Even granting that man shapes himself in a sense and to an extent that other animals do not, must we not acknowledge that such a process has to begin with something there to be shaped, and that the something prescribes boundaries or limits to the shaping?[15]

It is important to understand that humanists generally, and the historical school considered here in particular, have answered these questions in the affirmative. This fact has evidently puzzled sociobiologists because once it is admitted that, of course, man has a nature, they want to explore the question of what that nature is and how it produces Society and Culture. And the social scientist will have none of that and even considers the suggestion irrelevant. Why?

As we have seen, social theorists throughout Western history have by no means been averse to regarding man as an animal powerfully moved by organic dispositions. Attention to biological factors by sociologists and anthropologists has been, it can be argued, altogether too common.[16] As Teggart pointed out, with dismay, in 1918, "humanists in all branches of the study of man seem to feel it necessary to base their discussions upon what they

167

conceive to be the conclusions of modern biology."[17] The historical theorists discussed here, from Hume to Alland, have not denied the biological basis of human social life or even the possibility that biological differences among peoples are responsible for some part of the social and cultural differences they display. Existence of a human nature in that sense has not been seriously questioned. Human social and cultural histories could not have been lived by apes, and human beings could never have lived like apes. Humanists have known that they start with a given biological human being, and most would agree with Dobzhansky that there is no clear case for regarding the biological or genetic factor as negligible in the formation of culture and that it would be contrary to sound scientific procedure to assume in advance that there is no genetic basis of culture.[18]

The issue is not, then, whether humans have something called a nature. The point is that we do not, in the present state of knowledge, better understand human activities, and especially the differences among human activities, by looking for their source in human nature. Teggart argued from the plain observation that there has been no demonstration of biological differences among peoples that have operated in the production of cultural differences. Until biologists make such a demonstration (and this must properly be the work of biologists), it is, as Max Weber observed, the responsibility of social scientists to do everything they can with their own historical materials to explain and understand human social and cultural phenomena.[19] Or, as A. L. Kroeber put the matter, if we proceed on the assumption of a unity of human races in hereditary cultural capacity, then the problem of differences must be solved in other than hereditary terms—that is, in terms of historical and environmental factors. If, on the other hand, hereditary inequalities are demonstrated, then somebody has to ascertain the extent of differences attributable to historical and environmental influences if the effect of the hereditary factor is to be measured.[20]

What humanists have done in these circumstances is take man "as given" and proceed with historical explanations of his various social and cultural activities.[21] Humans are, obviously, capable of the activities in which we see them engaged. We do not know the ultimate sources of that capability, but we know from observation of the doings of animals and men that nonhumans do not have a capability for history-making and that humans do have it. It is in that sense given. Perforce it is assumed that all peoples have the same inherent cultural capacities, that there is a unity of the human race in this respect. To assume specific biological bases for human social and cultural activities is to stop historical analysis of differences in those activities. To assume, on the other hand, that people are everywhere, and at all times within the period of our historical information about them, the same, is to focus attention on cultural differences and to compel an explication of them. Here the idea of the psychic unity of mankind is neither dogma nor hypothesis. It is a working assumption in the study of cultural differences made necessary by the absence of knowledge that identifies different biological kinds of people and links the biological differences to cultural differences. In the course of their investigation of cultural diversity social scientists do not ignore information offered them by biologists. The information is not there. The working assumption of psychic unity is a necessity.

In accepting and defining society and culture as things in themselves, then, social scientists have been coming to grips with social and cultural activities of peoples, and this amounts to dealing with the different histories of peoples and the different results of those histories. Seeing man as something far more complicated than the abstraction that the economists and utilitarians had made of him involves putting man back into history.

This does not mean that humanity is lost sight of in the process or that an image of human nature entirely disappears. But the image takes a new form. Instead of being regarded as a derivation of universal organic traits, human nature itself is now viewed as a product of history in the sense of human activities, rather than history in the sense of biological evolution. That is all that is meant by the cryptic phrase, "Man makes himself."

As noted in chapter 4, a historical view of human nature was first clearly presented by Auguste Comte, and it is closely associated, of course, with his identification of the subject matter of sociology. Comte argued that human nature changes over historical time as a result of the accumulated experiences of successive generations. There is, therefore, no universal or abstract human nature, no human being as such, but only historical human beings. This, for Comte, was the same thing as saying that people are what they are by virtue of an ongoing social life. Comte could still argue, however, that this view of man as a product of social history in no way contradicts the fact that all social histories begin and proceed with a given human organism whose constitutional organization makes such social histories possible. Whatever happens in history, therefore, has to be in accord with the laws of human organization, but history could not be deduced from or understood in terms of that organization.[22]

Although argument continues about whether Marx and Engels had a concept of human nature with specific universal contents, it is nonetheless clear that they shared substantially Comte's opinion that man is significantly a product of his own activity. According to them, it is when people begin to produce their means of subsistence, when they appropriate nature's production, when they begin to labor, that they distinguish themselves from other animals and start to form their own nature. And again, for Marx and Engels, none of this is inconsistent with a materialist view that represents people's production of subsistence as "a step which is conditioned by their physical organization." Individuals "built on themselves" are just as real as physical individuals, for while individuals have built on themselves it has been "within their given historical conditions and relationships, not on the 'pure' individual in the sense of the ideologists."[23] Whether or not the labor process is to be regarded as the chief shaper of humanity, it should be observed that Marx and Engels were making the fundamental point that humans create their essential being in the historical actions of their social lives, and that this goes on in a hard, materialist setting.

This outlook on the relationship between human nature and sociocultural history was later refined and extended by the sociologist Émile Durkheim. He recognizes

171

the fact that when we speak of man we refer to a product of a civilizing process, that man differs from other animals in being civilized. To ask how man has come to be what he is, is the same, therefore, as to ask how civilization has come to be. So, it is "only by historical analysis that we can discover what makes up man, since it is only in the course of history that he is formed." Put in this way, Durkheim's alleged reification of society, his stark assertion of society's existence as a thing in itself, exterior to and constraining individuals, is modified into an empirical observation that people change in the course of historical time by virtue of their experiences.[24]

The suggestion in some of Durkheim's writing that the historical process creating man is uniform (the process of civilization) has more recently been modified by a reassertion of the pluralist view of history which characterized the work of Waitz, Teggart, and Toynbee. As George W. Stocking has pointed out, one of the key elements in the modern concept of culture is the idea that culture is generic inasmuch as it is present in the life of all peoples, and plural in the sense that it has different forms and contents while still retaining in each instance its integrity and its formative effects on persons.[25] Recognition of a historical dimension to human existence, as in Monboddo, or of a social component, as in Comte, has been easily accompanied by a conviction that all peoples eventually (if nothing interferes) come to shape themselves by the same general historical experience or that society everywhere exerts similar influences in making human nature what it is at any given stage of development. This is a form of historical or social or cultural determinism that shares qualities of rigidity and universalism with biological determinism.

If human beings are to be regarded as results of social and cultural experiences, however, the empirical-historical setting and course of the experiences must be respected. Peoples can have *kinds* of experiences, so that classification and comparison with a view to generalization is possible. But humans have never become humans by some abstract process of socialization, enculturation, or civilization. As Clifford Geertz has put it, persons become themselves as Dobuans or Javanese, Hopis or Italians, academicians or traders, not as some generalized culture product.[26]

While an image of human nature is retained, then, in the historical perspective, to perceive humans as products of time and place experiences in particular social and cultural settings is something different from seeing them as products of natural selection. The difference turns on the fact that the experiences and actions of people in the course of their social and cultural lives are not at all like the organic processes of variation, differential reproduction, and consequent modification of succeeding generations. To say that both sets of happenings are part of the experience of human beings and are therefore one, is to press reduction to the point of absurdity. Natural selection does not go on in such historical processes as cultural diffusion, challenge and response, disruption of custom and the release of individuals, invention and innovation, stratification, industrialization, or the social division of labor. These have taken place in the histories of peoples, and they have had their own effects. Their distinguishing feature is that they consist in acts of persons. If we determined precisely that natural selection had produced specified organic human attributes that are demonstrably responsible in some measure for such an array of happenings in human histories, that would be of interest in itself, but we would not thereby comprehend the operations and effects of the social and cultural activities involved. Clear demonstration of the operation of biological controls in the formation of social and cultural phenomena would always leave us with a need to account for variations in the effects and to isolate and measure historical influences in the process. Social and cultural histories are real and cannot be set aside as irrelevant to an understanding of human life. That is bad science, by any definition. To suppose that our undeniable ignorance about the complexities of human historical experience would somehow be relieved by disregarding the evidence of that experience and searching for its biological maker is to delude ourselves once more with the notion that there is an escape from historical empiricism by getting behind history and surprising the hand that moves it.

Considerations such as these moved Ortega y Gasset to remark that man has no nature—what he has is history.[27] This led some biologists to counter with warnings that historians must come to realize that what happens in history is a product of chromosomes shaped by natural selection.[28] Then Dobzhansky, in a spirit of moderation, suggested that man has both a nature and a history and that what we are given in experience is a result of interaction between the two.[29] This proposition has the sweet smell of reason about it, and it is supported by the striking case of a demonstrated relationship between human organic evolution and the history of tools. This seemingly judicious compromise can be misleading, however.

It obscures the integrity of human social and cultural histories by suggesting their basic dependence on biological controls. If the biological and cultural features of a human situation are distinguished quite clearly, and if the interaction between them is specified in an actual historical context, with historical evidence, the results can be significant and revealing, as the research on tools demonstrates. But if biological factors are viewed from the outset as ultimately determinative and cultural factors derivative or inconsequential, the results of inquiry about the interaction or interdependence have been fixed. Some biologists, as noted earlier, take the position that genetic factors determine what is most important in culture, and what they do not determine is incomprehensible to science. An area of the fortuitous or accidental is thus handed over for proximate historical accounting, while the substance of the matter is explained by allegedly "more structured" biological processes.

The unfortunate consequence of this ambiguity is a repetition of the retreat from human histories that has plagued the social sciences whenever biological or physical environmental explications of sociocultural phenomena have been advanced. The unsolved problem of distinguishing the innate from the learned in what humans do, combined with the readiness to reject that as a real question and to accept an intimate relationship or close likeness between the two, has led with dismal consistency to abandonment of the view that human social and cultural experiences are in themselves important formative influences on human beings. The result is what Kroeber spoke of as a "blind and bland shuttling back and forth" between organic and cultural explanations of

175

human activities, in which understanding of the reality of culture is blurred and lost.[30] This has as its usual effect a relaxation of efforts to unravel complications of historical events and a substitution of ultimate biological causes as explanations of sociocultural results.

There need be no implication in this argument that human biology must be ignored in the study of human social and cultural life. (Certainly there was no such implication in Kroeber's mind.) An avenue of exploration can be ruled out only with evidence bearing on specific, testable, propositions, and then only with respect to those particular claims. Again, the social scientist takes man as given because of a judgment that biologists have not actually revealed a human nature that accounts for or explains the facts of human histories nearly as well as social and cultural theories have. Social scientists can claim with justification that some biologists have maintained no such openmindedness on the question, but have assumed a fixed position that organic dispositions in man are the final, the ultimate, the significant determinants of all human history, except for those transient, ephemeral, fortuitous variations around basic themes.

That position involves saying, of course, that peoples have not really had histories in the sense in which Durkheim, Kroeber, and Ortega y Gasset used the term. It means saying, on the one hand, that any given set of social and cultural actions of a people are of no real importance for other social and cultural actions of that people or of other peoples. It also means that the different social and cultural actions of peoples are of no real importance intrinsically or for those peoples—that, to take Geertz's examples, it makes no difference to me whether human beings are Dobuans or Javanese, Hopis or Italians, academicians, or traders, and it makes no difference to them.

It is in light of the serious implications of such a view that Durkheim's social realism, Kroeber's designation of the superorganic, and Ortega y Gasset's denial of any such thing as human nature should be understood. Durkheim describes society as a "thing," and depicts its awful constraining power as some monstrous presence, in a deeply concerned effort to call attention to an order of actual occurrence that is being overlooked because it is so hard to define or measure or duplicate in the laboratory. The superorganic is made almost palpable by Kroeber, and it is strictly segregated from the organic, so that cultural things will not again be translated into biological things, as they have been, for example, in racial explanations of civilization. "Being" in man is rejected as a fiction and he is declared "infinitely plastic" by Ortega y Gasset in a desperate attempt to free us from the belief that change or becoming must be sought in immutable being. If these seem like overstatements, it should be remembered that they were made in the face of persistent attempts to set aside the evidence of historical experience as a molder of human conduct and install an organically constituted human nature in its place.

Continued efforts by biologists today to enlighten humanistic inquiry with yet another ontology of man have understandably evoked suspicions concerning political motivation. But the central issue is, again, the question of whether human beings have meaningful social and cultural experiences in which they, to some significant extent, make their history, or whether they are merely vehicles for biologically produced directors whose basic aim is reproductive fitness. The human sciences must be expected to continue to work from the former premise, not just on moral grounds, but on the hard evidence, contained in cultural differences, that human histories are real.

CHAPTER 7

ACTIVITY AND BEHAVIOR

Recognition of the fact that people have histories has provided, since at least the eighteenth century, a basis for humanistic inquiry and for distinguishing the study of man from the study of other parts of nature. The concept of history, in this context, carries a special meaning and should not be confused with the concept of time.

In the nineteenth century a revolution occurred in the natural sciences with the acceptance and development of the idea that the earth about us has had a history in the sense that its organic and geologic components have come into being and have changed through time. A belief in the existence of eternal and immutable forms that continue to manifest themselves in essential identities was replaced by a picture of the coming-to-be of all things from simple and homogeneous beginnings, through gradual natural processes, to the great complexity of differences observable in the present. This involved, eventually, total rejection of the notion that supernatural power had any part in the process. Everything

179

was comprehended as having had a history that would explain its present state or condition.

It has been noted often that this new conception of the natural world as a temporal process of change had long prevailed in Western thinking with regard to the human world of institutions, customs, arts, sciences, and so on. Conscious perception by Renaissance Europeans of the differences between themselves and classical antiquity in these respects was soon accompanied by a formal theory of change (the idea of progress) which purported to show how the later condition had grown out of the earlier. Apart from any consideration of the roots of this theory of cultural change in ancient thought, it should be clear that it did not derive from nineteenth-century natural science; enough has been said here and elsewhere to indicate how often a reverse borrowing prevailed.

There has been, nevertheless, a tendency to see the nineteenth-century acceptance of history as a general intellectual movement that cut across all lines of inquiry. Justification for this view certainly exists insofar as biologists and geologists did use ideas current among humanists and to the extent that students of human institutions such as law and religion felt sustained and encouraged in their historical approach by the recent success of what looked to some like a similar methodology in the natural sciences. Reimportation into the humanist disciplines of language borrowed by the life sciences, and adoption of newly coined natural scientific terms by anthropologists and sociologists, contributed to the impression that disciplined inquiry into all facets of human existence was marching ahead under a banner whose design was attributable chiefly to Charles Darwin.

When we say that all things that have come to be and have changed through time are therefore "in history" and are properly subjects of historical study, we perhaps do no violence to reality, but we do not facilitate coming to grips with its various aspects.

The history of sedimentary deposits or glacial effects in given areas encompasses time and place happenings. Similarly, the history of speciation in a given genus is made up of specific events. Geologists and biologists try to reconstruct the happenings or events from evidence, classify them into types or kinds, and relate classes by hypotheses. The idea of natural selection represents an attempt to account for sets of results in terms of a specified and measured relationship among events identified as the occurrence of variations of progeny from parents, the occurrence of differential reproduction by the various progeny, and the occurrence of the variations in the individuals so produced. Although we now speak of these related occurrences as a process and refer to the process generally as evolution, it is clear that we are talking about a number of events that have dates and loci. Biologists often refer to sets of such events as the evolutionary history of a kind of organism; and geological histories of a given formation or, more generally, of a given area, are common forms in which geologists report their investigations.

When we attend to human beings as a species, we recognize that they too, have had an evolutionary history in which the same kinds of events have taken place that occurred in the evolutionary histories of other organisms. We recognize, too, that the explanation by natural selection accounts for the results that we have before us in the human species insofar as those results fall into the class of organic phenomena that the theory was designed to explain.

Now when we move from this use of the term history to study the history of human social institutions or cultural elements it is clear that while we are still talking about happenings in time, the reference is to an order of events different from those seized by the idea of natural selection and therefore not explicable in its terms. This is simply to say that social institutions do not reproduce themselves, with or without variation, through anything like the *events* of organic reproduction. When we attend to the history of Gothic cathedrals, or the history of perspective in painting, or the history of steam calliopes it is evident that we are dealing with events that differ from the events that comprise the subject matter of the study of organic evolution. A commonsense description of the difference might be that Gothic cathedrals, paintings incorporating perspective, and steam calliopes are all products of human doing whereas the products of organic evolution are not. Put in another way, an event such as the construction of a Gothic vault differs from an event such as a mutation in that the former involves formation of intent or purpose on the part of an actor while the latter does not.

It is here, perhaps, that one can come to grips with the sociobiological proposition that ultimate explanation of happenings in human history is possible by the theory of natural selection. Gothic vaults, it could be said, do not in themselves have a history. We explain their presence by reference to the doings of persons. Such doings would have been impossible for organisms other than *Homo sapiens* because the evolutionary histories of other animals have not produced the attributes in them that human evolutionary history has produced in man. The attributes involved in the case of designing and building a complex arch might be specified as manual dexterity and intelligence. The ultimate historical explanation of Gothic vaults can therefore be regarded as an accounting for these human characteristics as products of natural selection. Now Gothic vaults assume the character of one among many and various manifestations of evolved human nature.

There is no gainsaying such a statement, of course, but as an explanation of how Gothic vaults came to be built it lacks specificity. Derivation of human doings from human nature is usually exemplified, therefore, in behaviors that are both more universal in time and space and more demonstrably tied to specific biological traits of limited function. It cannot be claimed that an organic disposition to build such things as arches has been isolated, described, and accounted for in terms of natural selection, but a serious case has been made for human dispositions to avoid incest or to protect and nurture kin. And there is little argument about the existence of specific organic foundations for many concrete human behaviors involving body care, comfort, sustenance, and reproduction.

But the contention that building Gothic vaults and snarling are both explicable as behaviors monitored by naturally selected organic controls is, on the one hand, an expression of a determination to uphold the idea of unity and continuity in nature. It is the same being that performs both acts, and there is no need, it is said, to postulate nonmaterial or supernatural forces to explain vault building just because we regard that as a loftier be-

183

havior than snarling. (Spiders and bees, after all, are skilled architects.) Man, it is argued, must be accepted as a unity, a natural unity, and this means recognizing the organic basis for all he does, just as we acknowledge the organic source of all behavior in other animals.

There is, on the other hand, an ambiguity in this picture of nature when the concrete evidence of human histories is confronted by sociobiologists. The concern to preserve the unity of nature against any non-natural elements is not, as we have seen, extended to an acceptance of everything that happens in human histories as comprehensible in natural terms. A category of the accidental or fortuitous is left open, not simply as a storage place for things of which we are presently ignorant, but as a bin into which behaviors not genetically controlled can be tossed. Such behaviors, for example, that express cultural differences within humankind are relegated to the class of unexplained trivia. And the entire course of human history that has resulted in an alleged discrepancy between human nature and modern civilization is also represented as a mistake that cannot be explained by natural selection.

This inability of some biologists to grasp and explain human histories derives fundamentally from a failure to tell the *difference between human activity and human behavior.* The fear that anything like a discontinuity in nature can be accounted for only in mystical or supernatural terms has resulted in an insistence on an absolute continuity between such doings as baring teeth and writing *The Origin of Species.* The result is that the distinguishing feature of human existence is either ignored or labeled as noise. Insistence by humanists on the special character of human histories and on the integrity and independence of human societies and human cultures is based on drawing a distinction between activity and behavior.[1]

Human activities are the conscious doings of people that go beyond and depart from both biological and traditional bonds. Human behavior is the routine doings of people that have become habitual and unexamined as a result of becoming fixed by biological and/or traditional controls. Ascertainment of biological bonds other than those involved in the simplest reflex movements is a difficult matter, and distinguishing biological from traditional controls when behavior is more complex has proved still more difficult. (The difficulty of this kind of analysis is, of course, no reason for abandoning an intrinsically interesting and significant line of investigation.) It is clear, nevertheless, from a comparison of sociocultural differences, that traditions—the customs of peoples and the sanctions enforcing them—are powerful shapers of habitual behavior. When, for any reason, the hold of tradition on a people is loosened, human activity becomes possible. Activity thus means the doing of something new and different, and it is responsible for sociocultural differences and for historical changes such as the appearance of what we call civilizations. Human activity is by no means limited to such unusual episodes, however, but is present in some measure and on some occasions in all societies. The contrast between activity and behavior is strikingly brought out when we notice the extremely rare and limited signs of activity in other animals.

A look at the way in which a recognition of human acitvity has arisen and has given the humanistic disciplines a perspective can serve as a summary, in somewhat different light, of the argument of this book.

The humanistic tradition in which people are regarded as capable of self-culture, able to make their own histories arose, it has been noted, in the course of a comparison of humans and other animals. It is not accurate to say that this is some dreamy vision of moral philosophers who were intent on buttering human vanity or making way for miraculous acts of utopia building. We have seen that this is a rather hardheaded idea, expressed with due regard to the material setting of human activities. When humans have been endowed with history-making powers to distinguish them from other animals, it has by no means always been with an intention of elevating them above the brutes, for, as the example of Rousseau reminds us, people have been regarded as quite capable of making rotten history for themselves.

It is, rather, the idea that a people's actions have consequences that underlies the expression that they make their history. Apart from the question of why acts are done—what the source or control or mediation of acts might be—it is of the utmost importance to understand that human actions in themselves result in real changes in conditions, in circumstances, and in the patterns of other actions by humans. Actions therefore explain such changes in the sense of accounting for them. Gothic vaults and polyphonic music and the Inquisition were new things that resulted from human activity. To say that the actions involved were intelligent or aggressive might be quite supportable, but it is not explanatory. George Washington stalked out of the United States Senate when the senators declined to discuss with him in advance a treaty he meant to negotiate. Washington's action and that of the senators were perhaps selfish, maybe aggressive, possibly spiteful; but certainly it is important to notice that those actions had concrete consequences for the manner in which United States foreign policy came to be conducted and for the results that followed from that conduct. Deciding to bomb Pearl Harbor and carrying out the decision were actions that had profound consequences in the lives of millions of people, and the consequences are understandable only in view of the specific shape and circumstances of those actions, not by identifying them as genetically monitored aggression or any other form of behavior.

To recognize the effectiveness of human actions does not, of course, require a belief that the results are those intended or expected by either the actors or other observers. Social scientists' emphasis on human activity as something *sui generis* does not imply that history is a pure expression of human will or that something comes out of nothing merely by a people's determination that it will be so. Nor should it be supposed that action goes on in a bland and uniform milieu so that results are nothing but functions of the action. As Marx reminded us, a group of men makes its own history, but they make it in circumstances given them by forces quite other than their own actions, and those circumstances powerfully affect outcomes. The point, then, is not that man's biology has nothing to do with his histories, nor that the physical environment has nothing to do with his social and cultural experiences, but rather that his activity in itself, however shaped or guided in part by organic and physical conditions, has its own consequences. *That* is what is being studied when humanists attend to the social and cultural experiences of peoples. When they are urged to look behind the activity to alleged genes or other biological forces that are supposed to produce it

187

they are in effect being told that they have taken an illusion as their subject matter. They are being told, to put it another way, that if they would understand what men do they must know what man is. Social scientists a century ago deliberately abandoned that perspective in favor of an orientation from which an understanding of what groups of people are involves knowing what they have done—what their histories are.

Appreciation of the significance of human activity as the shaper of human societies and cultures has been fostered by the observation that other animals do not form and alter the structure of their relations with their conspecifics or change the day-to-day and year-to-year doings of their kind. Other animals do not have histories in that sense. But other animals are not inert. Even casual observation of a beehive or a troop of monkeys reveals constant doings, and sophisticated ethologists portray a sometimes startling range of behaviors in their subjects. This is behavior, however, using the term to designate conduct that is fairly uniform throughout given age-grades and sexes in the species and that is constant over very long periods of evolutionary history. Apart from those rather isolated and limited instances of population-behavioral changes not attributable to biological changes (and, again, humanists should be deeply interested in systematic study of these), tigers and beavers and chimpanzees behave essentially as we have always known them to behave.

Why this is so is an interesting question on which biologists can no doubt shed light. Behaviors are regarded as products of natural selection, and since natural selection works very slowly (and may work to prevent change as well as promote it) we get the entirely accurate impression that the behavior of a species is constant. The question of why animals do not have behaviors that are not products of natural selection is harder.

If we look at human beings in this connection it is apparent that biologists are correct in pointing out behaviors that are fairly constant in time and space and are explicable in terms of natural selection. These include a variety of doings related to bodily functions clearly connected with survival and reproduction, and they are widespread and longstanding. They are discovered in both ancient and modern societies, and among existing industrial and hunter-gatherer societies. There is no difficulty here—no major disagreement about these facts among biologists and humanists. It would appear also that there are routine human behaviors that vary from one society to another and that must be explained, therefore, as adaptations to different environments or as results of different choices now congealed in tradition. These are the variations sometimes regarded as the trivia of cultural diversity, and they present the bothersome, but perhaps not crucial, problem of distinguishing between tradition and selection as sources.

When it comes to human activities, however, the evidence seems to compel explanation either in non-biological terms or by a thoroughgoing theory of biologically distinct groups in which gross differences in social and cultural lives are explained by corresponding and effective biological differences. The only alternative is to deny significance to the range of social and cultural differences displayed by historical records and the contemporary scene. Denial of differences is hardly tenable, even for sociobiologists, since they argue, as we have seen, that our terrifying predicament today stems from the fact that, while retaining a human nature formed long ago, we have become socially and culturally *different* from our hunter-gatherer forebears and contemporaries.

In this predicament it makes sense to suggest that while all peoples at all times have behaved in various traditional or similar biologically determined ways, there have been occasions when, for reasons we can expect to establish empirically, some peoples have acted outside of those customary and organic bounds with the result that new and different activity patterns have been created in place of or in addition to previous behavior.

The distinction between activity and behavior is most clearly discernible at the level of individual conduct. In the case of any individual in any human society the greater part of any day's or year's doing is routine. The body must be sustained. There is various pursuit to satisfy various craving. In a great number of ways an individual behaves half-consciously or unconsciously, in obedience to either custom or biological controls, to maintain himself in a social and a physical situation. What these ways are, how they have arisen, and what are their sources and present controls are difficult questions of interest to all students of humanity. But some of the time individuals act in situations not covered by either customary or biological controls and guidance. These are unusual, such as the circumstance in which old ways of defense against the usual predators do not work against a new threat for which new tools or tactics are demanded. Or there is a situation in which a stranger appears with a different food or implement or idea that calls for some assessment and, possibly, further action. Or there is an occasion when, for reasons of survival or aggrandizement, one moves out of accustomed grooves of work and must cope with novel procedures and with new competition. The passage of young persons out of familiar home surroundings into strange educational or work environments is a clear instance of moving from a behavioral situation into one where there is pressure for action. The colonist leaving his homeland, the youth marching off to war, the farm boy trying his luck in the city—all such are persons who have stepped over a margin on one side of which behavior was routine and on the other side of which some new action might be necessary and more new action is possible.

We know that societies in different times and places have confined persons in routine patterns of behavior to different degrees. To the extent that a social group is isolated from contacts with other, different groups, persons will be shielded from circumstances in which they can or must react in thought or deed to the new. Peoples whose physical situation has long exerted the same influence on conditions of livelihood are similarly shielded in their habitual behavior from new demands for action in work. Societies whose integrity or existence have not been threatened for a long time by other societies escape a major kind of stimulus to action and can safely move along customary lines of behavior. But when societies as such are shaken by intrusion or invasion by other and different peoples, passive behavior is difficult and the possibility of alternative conduct might be presented for the first time. Any new experience or change of condition opens possibilities for innovative activities, and the greater the contrast to a previous setting the more compelling the call for action.[2]

The question of whether individuals can be released

from *biological* controls and shift from behavior to activity in the course of historic disruptions of their life patterns is legitimate and interesting. Here once again it is very difficult, yet obviously necessary, to establish the fact of biological control in each instance where an answer to this question is sought. If biology can demonstrate such control in cases of empirically observed behavior, then it would be of interest to social scientists to look for historical circumstances under which the control might have been escaped and the behavior in question supplanted by conscious activity of another kind. Given the present state of biological knowledge in this area, however, the human sciences must be expected to deal with cases where demonstrated *customary* behavior has been transformed or replaced in disruptive situations by human activity.

The image of human beings altering their conduct under pressure of changed life conditions has often suggested to social theorists that here is a process of adaptation achieved by conscious or unconscious selection among available variations. Spencer worked out such a scheme, in different language, before Darwin published *The Origin of Species,* and it has been a favorite since.[3]

Sociobiologists today generally avoid this misleading use of "selection" and make it clear that they are talking about genetic bases of behavior that are produced by differential reproduction among bearers of random variations. Human social and cultural evolution from this point of view can be represented only as changing patterns of genetically directed behavior. But, as noted above, confusion on this point arises when cultural evolution sometimes is identified as nongenetic change and sometimes is regarded as resulting in part from genetic change and in part from chance. There follows from this much vague talk about the relationship of organic and cultural evolution, and even of an interaction between the two processes, as if what we are given in experience is not simply a congeries of happenings but rather two forces or constructors that make things happen.[4]

Whether social evolution is presented in its nineteenth-century Spencerian form or its twentieth-century sociobiological form, the reality of human activity is questioned. For the classical social evolutionists the process of development was so slow and gradual and inevitable that there was no room for acting humans to affect it. Spencer said that the best thing for people to do is avoid interfering with that beneficent process; scientific discovery of the course of evolution is useful, he believed, only for letting us know what we must not impede. Human progress, as Auguste Comte saw it, is to be described without reference to persons, or even peoples. Anything resembling a "great man" thesis is anathema in the house of social evolution.

The essence of sociobiology in this respect is a denial that the activities of persons have significance beyond the pressure they exert on evolutionary forces to bring activities back within genetically prescribed limits. In the language I have been using here, the tendency of sociobiologists is to reduce conceptually all human activities to human behavior. The point to be made is methodological, not moral. Whatever the implications of sociobiology for purposeful human acitivity, can the human social and cultural results that we see at any given time in the world be accounted for in all their variety if we do not recognize and attend to things people have done under the circumstances in which they have found themselves? That is the question posed by the thesis that human society and culture are *sui generis*. It is not an empty ontological question. It is a question of whether we shall accept human histories as relevant to explication of the conditions in which peoples everywhere are found. It is a question of whether the attempts by people to bring something about—the efforts of people—have been powerful influences in shaping human life conditions.

It is in an attempt to get at this singular feature of human life and to examine it with a view to better understand its manifold effects that humanists take biological man as given and proceed with explanations of sociocultural things in sociocultural terms. This is not to abandon reality and ultimate causes for illusion and ephemera. Human histories have had effects. Humanists study those effects. The effects of human biology in human sociocultural life have been, one must suppose, significant. But exactly what they have been and how they might be conceived to account for the variety of human experience has not been made evident.

It would be most interesting to be able to document a case where, in the evolutionary history of humans, changed circumstances of life could be connected with activity that produced changes in sociocultural items and related changes in biological make-up. Early tool-making and tool-using can be conceived as an innovative response to something new in the environment, and evidence and theory strongly suggest that this cultural element could then have become a term in the process of natural selection, with effects on hand and brain, to be followed by new sociocultural arrangements consequent on or made possible by such organic changes. Although biologists disagree on the matter, there is no compelling reason to reject the possibility of similar processes still going on. It is to be hoped that investigation of this sort continue and that it be productive. But even the most enthusiastic workers in the history of tools recognize the necessarily limited nature of their evidence and the limits thus imposed on the scope of their conclusions. Even if we can say that the making and use of tools started the processes of civilization, that leaves much to be said about human histories.

In taking man as given biologically, humanists are not, then, ruling out biological factors in human histories. They choose, rather, to recognize the very limited nature of the light biology can now cast on the activities of men, and they proceed to see what can be done by tending their own garden.

At a more general level, the picture of human experience presented by both social evolutionists and sociobiologists is the very antithesis of what historical records show. In place of a continuous process of sociocultural change, the records clearly indicate long periods of relative inactivity among peoples, punctuated by occasional spurts of action. Rather than slow and gradual change, significant alterations in peoples' experience have appeared suddenly, moved swiftly, and stopped abruptly. What we call civilization has been a rare and sporadic phenomenon in both space and time. Instead of the uniform or unilinear process of change that might be expected to result from a unity of genetic control within the species, where change has occurred it has obviously taken those manifold forms and produced those varied consequences that constitute the array of real cultural differences that history and ethnography reveal to us. Historical processes of sociocultural change are not an unfolding of some common potential, no hypertrophy of elementary forms. Changes appear in human social and cultural circumstances when something happens, when certain kinds of events occur and certain kinds of human actions are taken. The events leading to social change have occurred in the physical circumstances of social life, and the events immediately representing the change and leading to further social change have been the innovative activities of persons whose routine behavior has been disrupted by a breakdown of previously serviceable solutions to life problems. In this relationship of events the actions of a people are both responsive and creative; they are taken in specific circumstances and a new condition of human social and cultural existence results.

These relationships of kinds of physical and sociocultural events have been noted in the broad spectrum of historical investigations sampled in earlier chapters. The human sciences generally, however, proceed on the observation that the activities of men have consequences for the actual patterns of their social lives and the contents of their cultural lives. To the extent that humanistic inquiry is focused on problems of social order and cultural integrity, the conditions and circumstances of human inactivity are specified, and tradition-bound behavior is examined. There is every reason to explore and describe as well any biologically controlled behavior of this kind. Here the very practical matter of ongoing social relations necessary to human existence is investigated, and the functions of given cultural items for human life are described. Role-taking, symbolic interaction, ritual ceremonial performance, socialization, and the whole range of life-sustaining behaviors are the focus of attention.

When the problem of cultural differences is recognized, however, and the problem of cultural change necessarily along with it, questions distinct from those raised about system characteristics must be asked. Now the task is to find out how systems break down, how inactivity is succeeded by activity, and what the various outcomes of activity are. As these questions have been pursued it has become clear in a general way that episodes of human historical activity have been succeeded by another institutionalization of social life and another routinization of cultural work. Then the philosopher of history in each of us (not even sociobiologists are immune) is led to grapple with vexing questions of possible meaning in the successive phases of a single people's experience or, even more broadly, with composite pictures of the history of man.

Questions of destiny, of meaning in history, or of cosmic purpose are not likely to disappear from human discourse, and there are no legitimate grounds for proscribing them. A more immediate, and perhaps more practical, objective of historical study of social and cultural affairs, however, is a revelation of the kinds of lives peoples have so far led and the circumstances under which they have come to lead them. These are the alternatives displayed by cultural differences. Now it is obviously the case that knowledge of such differences is of no practical import if human beings cannot by their own activity make choices among alternatives and pursue alternatives. If the alternatives are essentially the same, and if what we regard as human activity is only a reflex consequent upon genetic signals, with no source or result in human activity itself, then the records of human histories are of little moment and study of them can yield only illusions. To deny the reality of human activity in this sense, then, is not only to put checkreins on freedom. It stops inquiry into historical sources of human conditions. It cuts man off from his history, denies him access to his experience.

When we notice that animals other than man do not have histories, we are not saying that they are in nature and man rises above nature. It is a fact of nature (if that word is useful) that human beings, in significant measure, have changed their ways and so themselves by their own actions. If we use the term human nature to name a kind of conduct of an interacting aggregate of people in an area during a time, then indeed there is such a thing as human nature and there is no point in debating whether man has a nature or a history. People *are* their histories. It is by their histories that they have come to be as we find them, in different societies, engaged in different behaviors and different activities.

NOTES

1. ANIMALS AND MEN

1. This is the specific proposal of Edward O. Wilson, *Sociobiology: The New Synthesis* (Cambridge, Mass.: The Belknap Press of Harvard University Press, 1975).

2. Charles Darwin, *The Descent of Man and Selection in Relation to Sex* (2d ed. [1874] Chicago and New York: Rand, McNally, 1974), pp. 112, 117, 613; Konrad Lorenz, *On Aggression*, trans. by Marjorie Kerr Wilson (New York: Bantam Books, 1967), ch. 12; Lorenz, *Studies in Animal and Human Behavior* (Cambridge, Mass.: Harvard University Press, 1970), 1:xiii–xiv. For similar views, see Theodosius Dobzhansky, *Heredity and the Nature of Man* (New York: Harcourt, Brace, and World, 1964), pp. 65–67; Cyril Dean Darlington, *The Evolution of Man and Society* (London: Allen and Unwin, 1969), p. 21; Stephen Jay Gould, *Ever Since Darwin* (New York: Norton, 1977), pp. 50, 267.

3. In this growing genre: Desmond Morris, *The Naked Ape* (New York: McGraw-Hill, 1967); Morris, *The Human Zoo* (New York: McGraw-Hill, 1969); Robert Ardrey, *African Genesis: A Personal Investigation into the Animal Origins and Nature of Man* (New York: Atheneum, 1961); Ardrey, *The Territorial Imperative* (New York: Atheneum, 1966); Ardrey, *The Social Con-*

tract (New York: Atheneum, 1970); Lionel Tiger, *Men in Groups* (New York: Random House, 1964); Lionel Tiger and Robin Fox, *The Imperial Animal* (New York: Holt, Rinehart, and Winston, 1971). Charming examples of the latitude possible in conjectural biological history: Joan Marble Cook, *In Defense of Homo Sapiens* (New York: Farrar, Straus, and Giroux, 1975); Elaine Morgan, *The Descent of Woman* (New York: Stein and Day, 1972).

4. Charles Darwin, *The Origin of Species* (6th ed. [1872]; New York: Collier Books, 1962), p. 414.

5. Aristotle, *Historia Animalium*, trans. by D'Arcy Wentworth Thompson; *The Works of Aristotle*, J. A. Smith and W. D. Ross, eds. (Oxford: Clarendon Press, 1949), 6:588b–589a. See also Aristotle, *Parts of Animals*, trans. by A. L. Peck; and Aristotle, *Movement of Animals; Progression of Animals*, trans. by E. S. Forster (London: William Heinemann, 1937), p. 333: "Nature passes in a continuous gradation from lifeless things to animals . . . with the result that one class is so close to the next that the difference seems infinitesimal."

6. *Politics*, in *The Basic Works of Aristotle*, Richard McKeon, ed. (New York: Random House, 1941), p. 1129.

7. Aristotle, *Parts of Animals*, p. 101.

8. Margaret T. Hodgen, *Early Anthropology in the Sixteenth and Seventeenth Centuries* (Philadelphia: University of Pennsylvania Press, 1964), pp. 415–17.

9. See Arthur O. Lovejoy, *The Great Chain of Being* (Cambridge, Mass.: Harvard University Press, 1942 [1936]).

10. I follow here the detailed and fascinating account compiled by Richard Bernheimer, *Wild Men in the Middle Ages* (New York: Octagon Books, 1970). Bernheimer says that figures like wild men appear throughout the history of Western civilization.

11. For an excellent history of the idea, see George Perrigo Conger, *Theories of Macrocosms and Microcosms in the History of Philosophy* (New York: Columbia University Press, 1922).

12. A remarkable use of such metaphor in description of plant "communities" and their parts and functions was devel-

oped in the early twentieth century by Frederic E. Clements. See *Research Methods in Ecology* [1905] (New York: Arno Press, 1977); Clements, *Plant Succession: An Analysis of the Development of Vegetation* (Washington, D.C.: Carnegie Institution, 1916); Clements and Glenn W. Goldsmith, *The Phytometer Method in Ecology* (Washington, D.C.: Carnegie Institution, 1924); Clements, John E. Weaver, and Herbert C. Hanson, *Plant Competition: An Analysis of Community Functions* (Washington, D.C.: Carnegie Institution, 1929).

13. Quoted in Hodgen, *Early Anthropology*, p. 394, from *Raleigh's History of the World*.

14. Eustace Mandeville Wetenhall Tillyard, *The Elizabethan World Picture* (London: Chatto & Windus, 1958 [1943]). Theodore Spencer, *Shakespeare and the Nature of Man* (2d ed.; New York: Macmillan, 1961).

15. Edward Tyson, *Orang-outang, sive Homo Sylvestris: or, the Anatomy of a Pygmie* (1699), facsimile with introduction by Ashley Montagu (London: Dawsons of Pall Mall, 1966), from "The Preface." "Orang-outang" was a general term in the seventeenth and eighteenth centuries for all apes.

16. *Ibid.*, p. 55.

17. *Ibid.*, p. 5.

18. *Ibid.*, from "The Epistle Dedicatory."

19. Hodgen, *Early Anthropology*, pp. 419–26, presents a convenient summary of these beginnings of European race theory.

20. A rich account of this enterprise in the Scottish Englightenment is presented by Gladys Bryson, *Man and Society: The Scottish Inquiry of the Eighteenth Century* (Princeton: Princeton University Press, 1945).

21. René Descartes, *A Discourse on Method* (London: J. M. Dent, 1912 [1637]), part 5, pp. 44–47.

22. *The Complete Works of Oliver Goldsmith* (London: 1825), 13:283, 292. Cf. Robinet (1768) who observed that the pongo and orang are "not truly men" but they fill a "transition from ape to man" and are connected with man by an "infinity of similarities." Quoted in A. O. Lovejoy, *Essays in the History of Ideas* (Baltimore: Johns Hopkins University Press, 1948), p. 52n.26.

23. *Buffon's Natural History* (Barr's Buffon) (10 vols.; London: Printed for the Proprietor, and sold by H. D. Symonds, 1807), 3:333.

24. Goldsmith, *Works*, 12:152; 13:278.

25. Lovejoy, *Essays*, p. 18n. 4.

26. Jean Jacques Rousseau, *The First and Second Discourses*, Roger D. Masters, ed.; trans. by Roger D. and Judith R. Masters (New York: St. Martins Press, 1964), pp. 92–95.

27. *Ibid.*, pp. 114–15.

28. *Ibid.*, p. 114.

29. *Ibid.*, p. 204.

30. *Ibid.*, pp. 207–8.

31. *Ibid.*, pp. 208–9. Rousseau's experiment is carried out in the novel by Vercors, *You Shall Know Them*, trans. by Rita Barisse (Boston: Little, Brown, 1953).

32. James Burnet (Lord Monboddo), *Of the Origin and Progress of Language* (6 vols.; Edinburgh: 1773–1792). The citations from volume 1 are from the second edition, "with large additions and correction" (Edinburgh: 1774); *Antient Metaphysics* (6 vols.; Edinburgh: 1779–1799).

33. Monboddo, *Language*, 1:313; *Metaphysics*, 3:337.

34. Monboddo, *Language*, 1:74.

35. *Ibid.*, pp. 24–25, 60, 75–76, 119–21, 135–38; Monboddo, *Metaphysics*, vol. 1, book 2, ch. 10; vol. 2, book 2, chs. 2–4; vol. 3, ch. 3 of Appendix.

36. Monboddo, *Language*, 1:182–83.

37. *Ibid.*, pp. v, 41, 95–96, 145–46, 149, 171, 186, 199, 367; Monboddo, *Metaphysics*, vol. 3, book 1, ch. 3, pp. 57, 282; 4:25–34; 5:323. Monboddo even introduced a "man the hunter" theme in this context, arguing that when necessity forced man to hunt, the wild beast part of him became predominant, war succeeded hunting, and he became fiercer than any other animal—when not subdued by laws and manners: *Language*, 1:396–98.

38. Monboddo, *Language*, 1:147–49, 231–34, 338–39, 417–26, 448, 457–58; *Metaphysics*, 1:131–33, 147; 6:288–90, 313 ff.

39. Monboddo, *Language*, 1:187–88, 194–95, 270–93, 297–98, 300–3, 334, 343 ff., 347–48, 359–60. Thomas Love Pea-

cock wrote an intricate novel in which the leading character is an orangutan: *Melincourt, or Sir Oran Haut-ton* (London: Macmillan, 1896). It was written in 1817 and published in 1818. Monboddo is quoted in footnotes throughout the book.

40. Monboddo, *Language*, 1:360–61; *Metaphysics*, 3:366 ff. Earl Count has argued that comparisons of man and animals, specifically, apes, did not shock the eighteenth century as they did the post-Darwinian nineteenth because in the later period a blood relationship was being asserted between man and ape while in the former the comparison was made only to demonstrate "certain consistencies of idea in a Deistic universe." "Evolution of the Race Idea in Modern Western Culture During the Period of the pre-Darwinian Nineteenth Century," *Transactions of the New York Academy of Sciences*, series 2, (1946), 8:149. There is no denying this distinction, but so far as shocking effect is concerned the details of the eighteenth-century comparison, including a fascination with sexual intercourse between humans and apes and the issue thereof, seem to serve a purpose other than illustration of "consistencies of idea."

41. A. O. Lovejoy argued that Monboddo was an organic evolutionist: "Monboddo and Rousseau," in *Essays*, pp. 38–61. Lia Formigari has recently made a similar case: "Language and Society in the Late Eighteenth Century," *Journal of the History of Ideas* (1974), 35:275–92. The interpretation of Bryson, *Man and Society*, pp. 67–77, is more convincing.

42. Monboddo, *Language*, 1:367.

43. *Ibid.*, p. 175.

44. *Ibid.*, p. 444. Monboddo seldom departed from his naturalism. Occasionally he would couple "God and nature" as agents, and he dabbled in the idea that if Providence had ever intervened in man's natural history it must have been in the invention of language. Monboddo, *Metaphysics*, 4:184–85.

45. Monboddo, *Language*, 1:iv, 25.

46. See George Boas, *The Happy Beast in French Thought of the Seventeenth Century* (Baltimore: Johns Hopkins University Press, 1933). Theriophily is apparent in the popular literature of ethology today. Besides items in n 3, see Emily Hahn, *On the Side of the Apes* (New York: Arena Books, 1972).

47. Thomas Huxley, *Man's Place in Nature and other An-*

thropology Essays (New York: Appleton, 1896). See esp. pp. 142, 151–56.

48. Bernard Mandeville, *The Fable of the Bees*, part 2 (London: 1729), p. 432.

49. *Ibid.*, pp. 146–47; Mandeville, *The Fable of the Bees: Or, Private Vices, Publick Benefits* (3d ed; London: 1724 [1714]), pp. 25–33, 256–57, et passim.

50. Bryson, *Man and Society*, p. 56.

51. David Hume, *A Treatise of Human Nature* (2 vols.; London: J. M. Dent, 1911 [1739–1740]), 2:47–50, 111, 112. Hume referred to swans, turkeys, peacocks, nightingales, horses, oxen, tigers, cats and, especially, dogs in this context, but the discussion is on an abstract level. He did observe, significantly, that one form of sympathy among dogs would be inexplicable to us "if we had not experience of a similar in ourselves." Early students of animal behavior displayed a candor that is not as evident in some of their scientific successors.

52. John L. Myres, *The Influence of Anthropology on the Course of Political Science*, University of California Publications in History (Berkeley: University of California Press, 1916), vol. 4, no. 1, p. 16.

53. Spencer, *Shakespeare*. Spencer is persuasive in attributing the power of Elizabethan drama to its confronting this basic question of contradictory elements in human nature.

54. Montaigne, "Apology for Raimond Sebond," in *The Essays of Montaigne*, trans. by E. J. Trechman (New York: Modern Library, 1946), pp. 379, 412.

55. *Ibid.*, pp. 382, 486, 509 ff.

56. *Ibid.*, p. 490.

57. *Ibid.*, pp. 381–84, 388, 398 ff., 410.

58. *Ibid.*, p. 395.

59. Ashley Montagu, *Man and Aggression* (2d ed.; London: Oxford University Press, 1973), pp. 3–18.

60. Quoted in George Boas, *Happy Beast*, p. 93.

61. Montaigne, "Apology" p. 388.

2. THE DARWINIAN HERITAGE

1. Charles Darwin, *The Origin of Species* (New York: Collier Books, 1962), p. 483.

2. THE DARWINIAN HERITAGE

2. George Gaylord Simpson, "The Biological Nature of Man," in S. L. Washburn and Phyllis C. Jay, eds., *Perspectives on Human Evolution: 1* (New York: Holt, Reinhart and Winston, 1968), pp. 2–3; originally in *Science* (1966), 152:472–78. Darwin himself would hardly have agreed. See, e.g., his reference to Shakespeare's "wonderful knowledge of the human mind." *The Expression of the Emotions in Man and Animals* [1872] (Chicago: University of Chicago Press, 1965), p. 365.

3. Richard Dawkins, *The Selfish Gene* (New York and Oxford: Oxford University Press, 1976), p. 1.

4. Julian Huxley, "The Emergence of Darwinism," in Sol Tax, ed., *Evolution after Darwin*, vol. 1: *The Evolution of Life* (Chicago: University of Chicago Press, 1960), p. 21.

5. Konrad Lorenz, *Studies in Animal and Human Behaviour*, trans. by Robert Martin (Cambridge, Mass.: Harvard University Press, 1970), 1:xii.

6. Michael T. Ghiselin, *The Economy of Nature and the Evolution of Sex* (Berkeley: University of California Press, 1974), pp. 216, 219.

7. For examples, see Kenneth Bock, "Darwin and Social Theory," *Philosophy of Science* (1955), 22:123–34.

8. The classic exposition is J. B. Bury, *The Idea of Progress* (London: Macmillan, 1928).

9. Darwin, *Origin of Species*, p. 213.

10. *Ibid.*, pp. 354–55.

11. *Ibid.*, p. 484.

12. Charles Darwin, *The Descent of Man and Selection in Relation to Sex* (2d ed. [1874]; Chicago and New York: Rand, McNally, 1974), p. 141.

13. Darwin also inserts "ancient men" (early Greeks and Romans, usually) into the series, but it is difficult to locate them in the list because they seem to occupy different positions with respect to different traits. This is true to some extent with all members of the series. The comparison of infants, the uneducated, and tribal peoples was, of course, an old ploy. Bernard Mandeville, among others, had observed that the "Vulgar," children, and savages do not have their human nature fully developed. *The Fable of the Bees*, part 2 (London: J. Roberts, 1729), p. 85.

205

14. Darwin, *Descent of Man*, pp. 14–15, 16–17, 19–20, 21, 37–38, 39, 50.

15. *Ibid.*, pp. 34–35, 74, 85, 91–93, 99, 106, 207, 356.

16. Darwin, *Expression of the Emotions*, pp. 13, 206, 244, 250.

17. *Ibid.*, pp. 294, 153–54, 264. Here and elsewhere it is clear that Darwin extended the series to discriminations among civilized males.

18. Darwin, *Descent of Man*, p. 107. Here, as so often in *Descent*, when Darwin was dealing with human social or cultural behavior, it seemed not to have occurred to him to support his statement with even a shred of evidence. The contrast with his biology is striking.

19. *Ibid.*, pp. 598–99. In establishing connections between man and other animals, and between civilized and savage man, Darwin was troubled by the facts that the progenitors of man were hairy and Europeans were a hairy people compared to some savages. He met the difficulty by attributing loss of hair in humans to sexual selection, and viewing hairiness in Europeans as a partial reversion. *Ibid.*, pp. 594–96.

20. Edward Burnett Tylor, *Primitive Culture*, 2 vols. [1871] (New York: Henry Holt, 1883; 3d American, from 2d English ed., 1873).

21. Darwin, *Descent of Man*, pp. 137–38.

22. *Ibid.*, pp. 26, 90–93, 113–16.

23. *Ibid.*, pp. 178–79, 183–85, 254n.

24. Tylor, *Primitive Culture*, 1:vii–viii, and J. F. McLennan, *Studies in Ancient History* (London: 1886, new ed.), p. xv, drew particular attention to the fact that they proceeded along lines different from Darwin's. T. H. Huxley also believed that the "progressive modification of civilization which passes by the name of the 'evolution of society', is, in fact, a process of an essentially different character, both from that which brings about the evolution of species, in the state of nature, and from that which gives rise to the evolution of varieties, in the state of art." T. H. Huxley and Julian Huxley, "Evolution and Ethics: (I) Prolegomena" [1894], in *Evolution and Ethics 1893–1943* (London: Pilot Press, 1947), p. 55.

25. Darwin, *Descent of Man*, p. 64.

26. Darwin, *Origin of Species*, p. 203; *Descent of Man*, pp. 144, 151–52.

27. See, e.g., Howard E. Gruber, *Darwin on Man; A Psychological Study of Scientific Creativity; Together with Darwin's Early and Unpublished Notebooks Transcribed and Annotated by Paul H. Barrett* (New York: Dutton, 1974), pp. xiv, 202 *et passim;* Stephen Jay Gould, *Ever Since Darwin: Reflections in Natural History* (New York: Norton, 1977), pp. 21–27.

28. Here is Engels, in a letter to Marx, one year before publication of *The Origin of Species:* "So much is certain; comparative physiology gives one a withering contempt for the idealistic exaltation of man over the other animals. At every step one bumps up against the most complete uniformity of structure with the rest of the mammals, and in its main features this uniformity extends to all vertebrates and even—less clearly—to insects, crustaceans, earthworms, etc." *Karl Marx and Friedrich Engels: Correspondence, 1846–1895. A Selection with Commentary and Notes,* trans. and ed. by Dona Torr (New York: International Publishers, 1934), p. 114. It is highly unlikely that Marx was shocked by this observation, any more than Engels was shocked by Darwin in the following year.

29. Darwin, *Descent of Man*, pp. 552, 558–59. For other observations on the sexes, see *ibid.,* pp. 559–60, 591–94, 599, 611.

30. *Ibid.,* pp. 112, 117.

31. *Ibid.,* p. 95n.

32. *Ibid.,* pp. 124–25, 129, 133, 138. It is curious that Darwin has been misinterpreted on this point. The *Descent* is clear about the existence of mentally inferior and superior peoples resulting mainly from natural selection. It has been suggested that Herbert Spencer misused Darwin to claim that the basic fitness of societies lies in their biology. See the Ann Arbor Science for the People Editorial Collective, *Biology as a Social Weapon* (Minneapolis: Burgess, 1977), pp. 41–42. For an interesting earlier exchange on Darwin's social Darwinism, see *Science and Society* (Spring 1941), 5(2):173–88; (Spring 1941), 5(4):373–75; (Winter 1942), 6(1):71–78.

33. Darwin, *Descent of Man*, p. 138. The qualities in men

that Darwin believed would enable one nation to prevail over others in the advance of civilization are intelligence, energy, bravery, patriotism, and benevolence.

34. *Ibid.*, pp. 174–75, 571; Darwin, *Expression of the Emotions*, p. 15.

35. Darwin faced a difficult problem here, and he did not actually resolve it. It is the problem of the evolution of altruism: how can behavior that is detrimental to an individual (e.g., benevolence or unselfishness), but serviceable to the group or society, be increased by natural selection? See *Descent of Man*, pp. 60, 127–29. Darwin actually suggested a possible answer in reciprocal altruism but relied mainly on a basic instinct of sympathy, itself a product of natural selection.

36. *Ibid.*, pp. 125, 129, 138.

37. *Ibid.*, pp. 129–30; Darwin, *Origin of Species*, pp. 216, 218.

38. Darwin, *Descent of Man*, p. 137.

39. *Ibid.*, p. 120.

40. *Ibid.*, pp. 120–21, 134, 137, 606, 612.

3. SOCIOBIOLOGY AND THE HUMAN SCIENCES

1. Theodosius Dobzhansky, *Mankind Evolving* (New Haven: Yale University Press, 1962), pp. 10, 21, 285; "The Biological Concept of Heredity as Applied to Man," in *The Nature and Transmission of the Genetic and Cultural Characteristics of Human Populations* (New York: Millbank Memorial Fund, 1957), p. 15; *Heredity and the Nature of Man* (New York: Harcourt, Brace, and World, 1964), pp. 4, 40–77.

2. A convenient historical review of the many ambitious efforts along this line appears in Pitirim Sorokin, *Contemporary Sociological Theories* (New York: Harper, 1928), chs. 4–7.

3. Edward O. Wilson, *Sociobiology: The New Synthesis* (Cambridge, Mass.: Belknap Press of Harvard University Press, 1975), p. 550.

4. Richard Lewontin, "The Human Animal," typescript, television production of WGBH-TV, Boston, Nova #410. First transmission, PBS, March 30, 1977, p. 17. See also, Lewontin, "Biological Determinism as a Social Weapon," in The Ann Arbor Science for the People Editorial Collective, *Biology as a*

Social Weapon (Minneapolis: Burgess, 1977), p. 15: "No evidence at all is presented for a genetic basis of these characteristics, [religion, warfare, cooperation,] and the arguments for their establishment by natural selection cannot be tested, since such arguments postulate hypothetical situations in human prehistory that are uncheckable." Stephen Jay Gould, another biologist, has similarly denied that there is "direct evidence for genetic control of specific human social behavior." *Ever Since Darwin: Reflections in Natural History* (New York: Norton, 1977), p. 254.

5. Edward O. Wilson, *On Human Nature* (Cambridge, Mass.: Harvard University Press, 1978), p. 46.

6. I cite here, for the basic theoretical literature, primarily Edward O. Wilson, *Sociobiology;* Wilson, *On Human Nature,* and David P. Barash, *Sociobiology and Behavior* (New York: Elsevier, 1977). See also, Richard Dawkins, *The Selfish Gene* (New York: Oxford University Press, 1976); Richard D. Alexander, "The Search for an Evolutionary Philosophy of Man," *Proceedings of the Royal Society of Victoria* (1971), 84:99–120; "The Evolution of Social Behavior," *Annual Review of Ecology and Systematics* (1974), 5:325–83; "The Search for a General Theory of Behavior," *Behavioral Science* (1975), 20:77–100; "Evolution, Human Behavior, and Determinism," *PSA 1976,* 2:3–21; M. J. West-Eberhard, "The Evolution of Social Behavior by Kin Selection," *Quarterly Review of Biology* (1975), 50:1–33; W. D. Hamilton, "The Genetical Evolution of Social Behaviour, I and II," *Journal of Theoretical Biology* (1964), 7:1–52; Robert L. Trivers, "The Evolution of Reciprocal Altruism," *Quarterly Review of Biology* (1971), 46:35–57; "Parental Investment and Sexual Selection," in B. G. Campbell, ed., *Sexual Selection and the Descent of Man, 1871–1971* (Chicago: Aldine, 1972), pp. 136–79; "Parent-offspring Conflict," *American Zoologist* (1974), 14:249–64; Trivers and Hope Hare, "Haplodiploidy and the Evolution of the Social Insects," *Science* (January 23, 1976), 191:249–63; Michael T. Ghiselin, *The Economy of Nature and the Evolution of Sex* (Berkeley: University of California Press, 1974). Useful collections of background literature and items from current controversy are: T. H. Clutton-Brock and Paul H. Harvey, eds., *Readings in Sociobiology* (San Francisco: W. H.

Freeman, 1978); Arthur L. Caplan, ed., *The Sociobiology Debate: Readings on Ethical and Scientific Issues* (New York: Harper and Row, 1978); Michael S. Gregory, et al., eds. *Sociobiology and Human Nature* (San Francisco: Jossey-Bass, 1978); Robin Fox, ed., *Biosocial Anthropology* (London: Malaby Press, 1975). Sociobiology is by no means all of a piece. Wilson is taken here as a strong spokesman, and Barash is accepted by Wilson as a serious representative of human sociobiology.

7. See the remarks of Wilson, *On Human Nature*, pp. 2, 13, 204–5.

8. *Ibid.*, pp. 55, 61, 97, 169.

9. *Ibid.*, pp. 32–34. Variations on this position are introduced by considerations of reciprocal altruism. See Trivers, "Reciprocal Altruism."

10. The ethical question is treated by Wilson, *Sociobiology*, ch. 1 and pp. 562–64; *On Human Nature*, ch. 1, 9 and pp. 96–97, 119–20; Dawkins, *Selfish Gene*, pp. 3, 215. Barash is careful with the subject, but he would not be surprised "if unconscious fitness considerations were the ultimate underlying source of these judgements," p. 235. Ghiselin, *Economy of Nature*, p. 263, believes that intellect can raise us above our own base nature and "develop ethical standards consistent with biological reality." For other recent discussions, see Derek Freeman, "Human Nature and Culture," in *Man and the New Biology: The University Lectures, 1969, Australian National University* (Canberra: Australian National University Press, 1970); Donald T. Campbell, "On the Conflicts between Biological and Social Evolution and between Psychology and Moral Tradition," *American Psychologist* (December 1975), pp. 1103–26. The subject is, of course, an old one. See, T. H. Huxley and Julian Huxley, *Evolution and Ethics: 1893–1943* (London: Pilot Press, 1947), pp. 1–32, where Julian Huxley presents a concise history of the search for a naturalistic ethic; L. T. Hobhouse, *Morals in Evolution* (New York: Holt, 1906); Edward Westermarck, *The Origin and Development of the Moral Ideas* (2d ed., 2 vols; London: Macmillan, 1924–1926 [1906–1908].

11. Wilson, *On Human Nature*, pp. 13, 78.

12. Wilson, *Sociobiology*, p. 550.

13. For example, Michael T. Ghiselin, *Economy of Nature*.

3. SOCIOBIOLOGY AND THE HUMAN SCIENCES

14. It has not been difficult to make a case that sociobiologists get their conception of human nature from the traditional humanistic literature, and not from scientific inquiry. See Marshall Sahlins, *The Use and Abuse of Biology: An Anthropological Critique of Sociobiology* (Ann Arbor: University of Michigan Press, 1976). Ghiselin, *Economy of Nature*, is candid about getting his views on human nature from Adam Smith.

15. Barash, *Sociobiology and Behavior*, p. 288.

16. This is the way it is put by Dawkins, *The Selfish Gene*, p. 21, and by Wilson, *Sociobiology*, p. 3.

17. These examples are drawn chiefly from Wilson, *On Human Nature*, pp. 36–50 and chs. 5, 7, 8. See also Joseph Shepher, "Mate Selection among Second Generation Kibbutz Adolescents and Adults: Incest Avoidance and Negative Imprinting," *Archives of Sexual Behavior* (1971), 1:293–307; William H. Durham, "Resource Competition and Human Aggression, Part I: A Review of Primitive War," *Quarterly Review of Biology* (1976), 51:385–415; Seymour Parker, "The Precultural Basis of the Incest Taboo: Toward a Biosocial Theory," *American Anthropologist* (1976), 78:283–305; John Hartung, "On Natural Selection and the Inheritance of Wealth," *Current Anthropology* (1976), 17:607–22.

18. These and other intriguing suggestions are presented by Barash, *Sociobiology and Behavior*, ch. 10. See also P. L. van den Berghe and D. P. Barash, "Inclusive Fitness and Human Family Structure," *American Anthropologist* (1977), 79:809–23. Explorations of this sort tied more closely to actual populations and to more specific behavior are Melvin J. Konner, "Aspects of the Developmental Ethology of a Foraging People," in N. Blurton-Jones, ed., *Ethological Studies of Child Behavior* (Cambridge: Cambridge University Press, 1972), pp. 285–304; S. H. Katz, M. L. Hediger, and L. A. Valleroy, "Traditional Maize Processing Techniques in the New World," *Science* (1974), 184:765–73.

19. Wilson reviews the data in *On Human Nature*, pp. 43–46.

20. William H. Durham, "Resource Competition." A relationship between protein and primitive warfare has been ques-

tioned by Napoleon A. Chagnon and Raymond B. Hames, "Protein Deficiency and Tribal Warfare in Amazonia: New Data," *Science* (1979), 203:910–13. Even in nonhuman sociobiology the population data are often meager. But for a striking exception see Paul W. Sherman, "Nepotism and the Evolution of Alarm Calls," *Science* (1977), 197:1246–53.

21. Wilson, *On Human Nature*, p. 33. This idea is given rather strained expression in the observation that "sociobiological theory can be obeyed by purely cultural behavior as well as by genetically constrained behavior." Barash also clearly recognizes that cultural traditions shape adaptive behavior, *Sociobiology and Behavior*, pp. 268, 281–83. Theodosius Dobzhansky noted simply that culture is "an extrabiological method of adaptation." *Mankind Evolving*, p. 223. A more detailed analysis of this phenomenon was earlier presented by Fred A. Mettler, *Culture and the Structural Evolution of the Neural System*. James Arthur lecture on the evolution of the human brain, 1955 (New York: American Museum of Natural History, 1956), pp. 34–35.

22. Wilson's discussion of the problem of genetic determination is in *On Human Nature*, pp. 19–51.

23. As Earl Count put it: "None of Lorenz' human considerations have the same painstaking inquiry [as his bird studies] behind them; they amount to a kind of extrapolation from the concepts obtained from nonhumans." "Beyond Anthropology: Toward a Man-Science," *American Anthropologist* (1972), 74:1359.

24. Richard Alexander, "Evolution, Human Behavior," p. 6. For an illustration of the misunderstandings that can arise in this connection see William H. Durham, *Resource Competition*, where he undertakes to show that, contrary to the view that warfare is not adaptive, it can actually be highly adaptive in terms of survival and reproduction. The "clinical" interpretation of war as a useless and harmful aberration has been vigorously opposed by social scientists who have clearly pointed out real advantages secured by waging war, and who have done so entirely on the basis of historical observations, not genetic considerations.

212

3. SOCIOBIOLOGY AND THE HUMAN SCIENCES

25. Wilson, *On Human Nature*, pp. 16–17.

26. *Ibid.*, p. 40.

27. *Ibid.*, pp. 34, 88, 146.

28. *Ibid.*, p. 216. Dobzhansky, *Mankind Evolving*, p. 319, got himself into a similar predicament when he remarked that most changes in social and cultural life "occurred not because human populations were altered genetically, but because they were altered culturally."

29. The separation of cultural reality into areas that can be understood in proximate terms (by social scientists) and ultimate terms (by biologists) is a characteristic of much of sociobiological analysis. See especially, Barash, *Sociobiology and Behavior*.

30. The specific form of Lorenz's argument was presented by Thomas Huxley in his Romanes lecture of 1893. See T. H. Huxley and Julian Huxley, *Evolution and Ethics: 1893–1943* (London: The Pilot Press, 1947), p. 64. And the idea was there in one of Darwin's early notebooks where he observed that instincts such as revenge and anger might at one time have been necessary for man but had now better be checked. "Our descent, then, is the origin of our evil passions!!—The Devil under the form of Baboon is our grandfather!" "M Notebook," pp. 122–23, in Howard E. Gruber, *Darwin on Man* (New York: E. P. Dutton, 1974), p. 289.

31. Dobzhansky, *Mankind Evolving*, p. 210, creates a similar problem of measurement when he says that the evolution of culture has transformed "man's way of life" in the last 5,000 years more than biological evolution has in more than 50,000 years.

32. Wilson's discussion of the relationship of biological and cultural evolution appears in *On Human Nature*, pp. 78–80. See also, Barash, *Sociobiology and Behavior*, pp. 311–12, 318–24.

33. Thelma Rowell, "How Would We Know if Social Organization Were Not Adaptive," in Irwin S. Bernstein and Euclid O. Smith, eds., *Primate Ecology and Human Origins* (New York: Garland, in press).

34. Wilson, *On Human Nature*, p. x.

35. Barash, *Sociobiology and Behavior,* pp. xi, 54, 61, 276–77, 315.
    36. Dawkins, *The Selfish Gene.*
    37. See Wilson, *On Human Nature,* pp. 1, 175, 191; Ghiselin, *Economy of Nature,* pp. 13–24, 31, 216–19, 222. My contention here and throughout that biologists have been, and are, unduly concerned with humanists' beliefs about free will, the soul, and the special divinity of man should be tempered with an acknowledgment, first, that the William Jennings Bryan opposition to Darwinism is still with us, and, second, that a small group of religious social scientists continues to resist the "extreme principle of evolution." On the first point, see Richard D. Alexander, "Evolution, Creation, and Biology Teaching," *The American Biology Teacher* (1978), 40:91–107. On the second, see A. Irving Hallowell, "The Structural and Functional Dimensions of a Human Existence," in M. F. Ashley Montagu, ed., *Culture and the Evolution of Man* (New York: Oxford University Press, 1962), pp. 229–30. But neither of these groups is strongly represented in scholarly enterprise; and the issue raised by a search for an understanding of human social life in the biology of human nature does not turn on the kind of arguments they make.

4. HUMAN NATURE AND CULTURAL DIFFERENCES

1. See Eric H. Armington, ed., *Greek Geography* (London: Dent, 1934). Herodotus stands as a notable exception to this pattern of classical thought. He tried to explain customs and habits of peoples not only by their physical surroundings but as products of particular historical experiences, especially their contacts with alien cultures.
    2. Jean Bodin, *Six Bookes of a Commonweale* [1576], book 5, ch. 1. Charles Montesquieu, *The Spirit of Laws* [1748], book 14. In both classical and modern environmental explanations of human differences the argument was, of course, for the direct influence of environment on persons. For a review of the history of environmentalism, with bibliography, see O. H. K. Spate, "Environmentalism," in David L. Sills, ed., *International Encyclopedia of the Social Sciences* (New York: Free Press, 1968), 5:93–97.

4. HUMAN NATURE AND CULTURAL DIFFERENCES

3. A history of the monogenist-polygenist debate in the sixteenth and seventeenth centuries, with relevant documents, appears in T. Bendyshe, "The History of Anthropology" in *Memoirs Read before the Anthropological Society of London*, vol. 1 (1863–1864) (London: Trubner, 1865).

4. As noted in chapter 1, Sir William Petty, *The Scale of Creatures* (1676–1677) and Linnaeus, *System of Nature* (1735). A rare occurrence of race theory in the eighteenth-century era of uniformitarianism is Lord Kames (Henry Home), *Sketches of the History of Man* (Edinburgh, 1774).

5. Aristotle dealt with these questions throughout his writings, but see, especially, *Physics*, 2:1–8; *Politics*, 1:2, 2:8.

6. Daniel Defoe, *The Life and Strange Adventures of Robinson Crusoe* [1719] (Garden City, N.Y.: Doubleday, Doran, n.d.), part 1, pp. 235–36.

7. Turgot, "Plan de deux discours sur l'histoire universelle," in Gustave Schelle, ed., *Oeuvres de Turgot et documents le concernant, avec biographie et notes* (Paris: F. Alcan, 1913), 1:304.

8. A classic account of this quest and its implications is Carl Becker's *Heavenly City of the Eighteenth Century Philosophers* (New Haven: Yale University Press, 1932).

9. This idea was close to the belief that basic racial differences produced cultural differences, and early cultural evolutionists were reluctant to pursue that line of thought because it ran counter to their picture of mankind as a unity. If there were different kinds of people in the world, then identification of a single historical process in which all peoples participated would be difficult, and the search for a natural morality common to all men, discouraging.

10. Auguste Comte, *Cours de Philosophie Positive*, 4ᵉ ed. (Paris, 1877), 4:328; 5:6–7, 12–17.

11. Bernard Mandeville, *The Fable of the Bees*, part 2 (London, 1729), pp. 67, 133, 156.

12. Adam Smith, *The Wealth of Nations* (1776). This statement appears in the opening paragraph of book 1, ch. 1, "Of the Principle which Gives Occasion to the Division of Labor." Adam Ferguson, *An Essay on the History of Civil Society* [1767] (8th ed.; Philadelphia: 1819), pp. 11–12.

4. HUMAN NATURE AND CULTURAL DIFFERENCES

13. Élie Halévy offers a superb analysis of Bentham and the utilitarian tradition in *The Growth of Philosophic Radicalism,* trans. by Mary Morris (London: Faber & Faber, 1949).

14. David Hume, *An Enquiry Concerning Human Understanding* (Oxford: Clarendon Press, 1975), p. 83.

15. Auguste Comte, "Plan of the Scientific Operations Necessary for Reorganizing Society," in *System of Positive Polity,* trans. by John H. Bridges, et al. (London: 1875–1877), 4:558, 581–84.

16. Lewis Henry Morgan, *Ancient Society, or Researches in the Lines of Human Progress from Savagery through Barbarism to Civilization* (New York: Henry Holt, 1877), pp. 37, 40, 50, 59, 60, 61, 425. Condorcet had earlier suggested that the perfectibility of man is apparent not only in his improved intellectual and moral conduct, but also in the faculties or organization upon which intellectual and moral activities depend. Thus man improves himself by education, but education enhances his powers for such improvement, and *both* products are transmitted to his progeny. Progress is thus doubly assured. *Outlines of an Historical View of the Progress of the Human Mind,* trans. from the French (London: printed for J. Johnson, 1795), pp. 366–72.

17. Frederick Engels, "The Part Played by Labour in the Transition from Ape to Man," [1876] in *Dialectics of Nature,* trans. and ed. by Clemens Dutt (New York: International Publishers, 1960), pp. 279–96.

18. Morgan, *Ancient Society,* pp. 17–18, 61, 398; Karl Marx, *Capital* (Chicago: Charles H. Kerr, 1906), 1:13.

19. This was the basic problem of Edward Burnett Tylor's *Researches into the Early History of Mankind and the Development of Civilization* (London: 1865). Cultural evolutionists looking for purely evolutionary processes of change were interested in finding instances of "independent" development.

20. This was actually a return to an earlier position—to explain cultural similarities in terms of diffusion instead of in terms of common human nature or universal time processes. The spread of human populations carrying an original common culture after the flood had been an acceptable picture to Europeans.

21. See Paul Radin, *The Method and Theory of Ethnology, An Essay in Criticism* (New York: McGraw-Hill, 1933), pp. xi–xiii, et passim.

22. The search for what is common or universal in human cultures was called for specifically by Clark Wissler, *Man and Culture* (New York: Thomas Y. Crowell, 1923), ch. 12; George Peter Murdock, "The Common Denominator of Cultures," in Ralph Linton, ed., *The Science of Man in the World Crisis* (New York: Columbia University Press, 1945), pp. 123–42; Clyde Kluckhohn, "Universal Categories of Culture," in A. L. Kroeber, ed., *Anthropology Today* (Chicago: University of Chicago Press, 1953), pp. 507–23; Robin Fox, *Encounter with Anthropology* (New York: Harcourt Brace Janovich, 1973), pp. 311–39. Fox is pleading the cause of structuralists who seek those features of human nature that determine cultural possibilities. Fox is quite aware that this represents a return to an eighteenth-century objective.

23. Friedrich Hertz, *Race and Civilization*, trans. by A. S. Levetus and W. Entz (New York: Macmillan, 1928), p. 311: "Race theories are little else but the ideological disguises of the dominators' and exploiters' interests." On this and other aspects of the history of race theory, see Jacques Barzun, *Race: A Study in Superstition* (rev. ed., New York: Harper and Row, 1965); Ruth Benedict, *Race: Science and Politics* (New York: Modern Age Books, 1940); Oliver Cromwell Cox, *Caste, Class, and Race* (New York: Doubleday, 1948); M. F. Ashley Montagu, *Man's Most Dangerous Myth: The Fallacy of Race* (3d ed.; New York: Harper, 1952); John S. Haller, Jr. *Outcasts from Evolution: Scientific Attitudes of Racial Inferiority, 1859–1900* (Urbana: University of Illinois Press, 1971); Kenneth A. R. Kennedy, *Human Variation in Space and Time* (Dubuque, Iowa: Wm. C. Brown, 1976); Earl W. Count, "The Evolution of the Race Idea in Modern Western Culture During the Period of the Pre-Darwinian Nineteenth Century," *Transactions of the New York Academy of Sciences* (1946), series 2, vol. 8, pp. 139–65; Earl W. Count, ed., *This is Race: An Anthology Selected from the International Literature on the Races of Man* (New York: Schuman, 1950).

24. Thus Henry Sumner Maine: ". . . these assertions of an

ineradicable difference between the different races of mankind belong to a now exploded philosophy." "Memorandum on the Caird Report," in M. E. Grant Duff, *Sir Henry Maine, A Brief Memoir of His Life* (London: John Murray, 1892), p. 428. "It is to be hoped that contemporary thought will before long make an effort to emancipate itself from those habits of levity in adopting theories of race which it seems to have contracted." *Lectures on the Early History of Institutions* [1875] (3d ed.; London: John Murray, 1880), p. 96.

25. It is misleading to suppose that humanist resistance to a Darwinian social science results from holding Darwin responsible for the excesses of social Darwinism. No knowledgeable social theorist is likely to credit Darwin with innovation in an area where his indebtedness to social theory is so much more apparent. That the authority of Darwin's science was used to support an old and established doctrine is, at the same time, clear. Biologists are obliged to take care if their theories are not to be used for ideological purposes.

26. For examples of this sort of misinterpretation, see Kenneth Bock, "Comparison of Histories: The Contribution of Henry Maine," *Comparative Studies in Society and History* (1974), 16:236–37.

27. Theodosius Dobzhansky put the problem this way: "[natural] selection tends to increase Darwinian fitness; Darwinian fitness is reproductive fitness, not necessarily fitness for social progress." This does not mean, as Dobzhansky also observed, that natural selection has not produced wisdom or fitness for social life. *Mankind Evolving: The Evolution of the Human Species* (New Haven: Yale University Press, 1962), pp. 129, 330.

28. Charles Darwin, *Descent of Man and Selection in Relation to Sex* (2d ed. [1874] Chicago: Rand, McNally, 1974). ch. 5. When Darwin spoke of progressive and backward peoples he was referring, objectively, only to cultural differences and was faced with the problem of differences. He saw cultural differences in the light of the idea of progress.

29. Edward O. Wilson, *Sociobiology: The New Synthesis* (Cambridge, Mass.: Belknap Press of Harvard University Press,

1975), p. 548; *On Human Nature* (Cambridge, Mass.: Harvard University Press, 1978), pp. 18–19, 21, 73.

30. Wilson, *On Human Nature*, pp. 33, 67, 79, 167.

31. *Ibid.*, pp. 88–89, 207, ch. 5, 6.

32. *Ibid.*, pp. 128–29; Irven DeVore and Scot Morris, "The New Science of Genetic Self-Interest," *Psychology Today* (February 1977), p. 88. The decision to take cultural similarities rather than differences as the phenomena calling for explanation is a traditional orientation characteristic of Western Europeans who have sought to deny or tame the strange in alien cultures by assimilating it to the familiar and safe dimensions of their own culture.

33. Wilson is struck by the "protean ethnicity" of man. *Sociobiology*, p. 548. DeVore remarks the "enormous variety of cultural contexts," but believes that this only demonstrates the strength of the genetic element that maintains the panhuman under such pressure. (DeVore and Morris, "Genetic Self-Interest," p. 88.) One is reminded of Auguste Comte's argument that the progressive principle in history must be very strong to have withstood a prevalence of stagnation and retrogression.

34. The given human nature might be changed, according to Wilson, but he regards that as a distant possibility awaiting developments in genetic engineering. *On Human Nature*, pp. 97, 208.

35. Wilson, *Sociobiology*, p. 559; *On Human Nature*, p. 207.

36. Wilson, *On Human Nature*, pp. 1, 114–16, 132, 156.

37. *Ibid.*, p. 153, Wilson, *Sociobiology*, pp. 550, 559.

38. Wilson, *Sociobiology*, p. 550.

39. Wilson, letter in *New York Times Magazine* (Nov. 30, 1975), p. 86; *On Human Nature*, pp. 42–43, 46.

40. Wilson, *On Human Nature*, pp. 48, 50.

41. Wilson, *Sociobiology*, p. 550.

42. Wilson, *On Human Nature*, pp. 153–54.

43. DeVore says that "Sociobiology doesn't need recourse to genetic differences between individuals to explain behavioral differences. The primary thrust is to explain behavioral differences as adaptive responses to environmental differences." (DeVore and Morris, "Genetic Self-Interest," p. 86.) He must

have in mind here a process of adaptation that involves no genetic change.

44. Darwin, *Descent*, p. 137.

5. HISTORY AND CULTURAL DIFFERENCES

1. David Hume, "Of the Rise and Progress of the Arts and Sciences" (1742) and "Of National Characters" (1748), in *Essays: Moral, Political, and Literary* (London: Grant Richards, 1903), pp. 112–38, 202–21.

2. James Dunbar, *Essays on the History of Mankind in Rude and Cultivated Ages* (2d ed; London: 1781). See esp. pp. 174–75, 179–90, 421, 425, 432–33, 436.

3. *The Anthropological Treatises of Johann Friedrich Blumenbach*, trans. and ed. by Thomas Bendyshe (London: Longman, Green, 1865 [1775; 3d ed. 1795]), p. 98.

4. Hugh Murray, *Enquiries Historical and Moral, Respecting the Character of Nations* (Edinburgh: J. Ballantine, 1808). See esp. pp. 12–13, 21–22, 36–37, 109–10. Murray, although fully aware that what he called progress was a relatively rare phenomenon and consequent only on particular conditions, went on to present a general history of human progress by constructing a developing series from the different tribes and nations known to him. When he used the contemporary "savage" as a historical document in this procedure, however, he saw that he was then engaged in conjecture, not history. And he showed a general uneasiness with this use of the comparative method, as distinguished from his comparison of histories for the purpose of accounting for differences. See pp. 165–66, 330–31.

5. George Cornewall Lewis, *A Treatise on the Methods of Observation and Reasoning in Politics* (2 vols.; London: Parker, 1852), 1:38, 302–5.

6. *Ibid.*, 2:429–31, 434–35.

7. Theodor Waitz, *Introduction to Anthropology*, ed. by J. Frederick Collingwood from the first volume of *Anthropologie der Naturvolkes* (London: Longman, Green, Longman, and Roberts, 1863). Darwin had read Waitz before writing *Descent* in 1871, but cites him only for some ethnographic data.

8. Some of the literature on race cited by Waitz in this connection: Charles Hamilton Smith, *Natural History of the*

Human Species (Edinburgh: Lizars, 1848); Josiah Clark Nott and George R. Gliddon, *Indigenous Races of the Earth* (Philadelphia: Lippincott, 1857); Nott and Gliddon, *Types of Mankind* (Philadelphia: Lippincott, Grambo, 1855); Alexander Agassiz, "Christian Examiner" (Boston: July 1850); Robert Knox, *The Races of Man* (London: Renshaw, 1850); Samuel George Morton, *Crania Americana* (Philadelphia: Dobson, 1839); Morton, *Crania Aegyptica* (Philadelphia: Penington, 1844); Morton, *Some Observations on the Ethnography and Archaeology of the American Aborigines* (New Haven: Printed by B. L. Hamlen, 1846); Morton, *Hybridity in Animals and Plants* (New Haven: B. L. Hamlen, 1847); Peyroux de la Coudrenière, *Mémoire sur les sept espèces d'Hommes* (Paris: Allut, 1814); Gustav Klemm, *Allgemeine Culturgeschichte der Menschheit*, 10 vols. (Leipzig: Teubner, 1843–51); Adolf Wuttke, *Geschichte des Heidentheums*, 2 vols. (Breslau: J. Max, 1852–53).

9. Waitz, *Introduction*, p. 1.

10. *Ibid.*, pp. 289–91, 312, 381.

11. For a summary of Waitz's conclusions in this area see *ibid.*, pp. 229–30.

12. *Ibid.*, pp. 260, 329.

13. *Ibid.*, pp. 328–50.

14. *Ibid.*, pp. 8, 351.

15. *Ibid.*, pp. 380–81.

16. *Ibid.*, pp. 382–89.

17. Among the German historical jurists: Gustav Hugo, Karl Friedrich Eichorn, Friedrich Carl von Savigny. Henry Sumner Maine's principal works: *Ancient Law* (London: John Murray, 1861); *Dissertations on Early Law and Custom* (New York: Henry Holt, 1883); *Lectures on the Early History of Institutions* (London: John Murray, 1875); *Village-Communities in the East and West* (London: John Murray, 1871).

18. Quoted on the frontispiece of Paul Radin's *The Method and Theory of Ethnology* (New York: McGraw Hill, 1933).

19. Franz Boas, *The Mind of Primitive Man* (New York: Macmillan, 1911), pp. 6–17.

20. Teggart presented his views on this subject in *Prolegomena to History* (Berkeley: University of California Press, 1916); *Processes of History* (New Haven: Yale University Press,

1918); and *Theory of History* (New Haven: Yale University Press, 1925). The latter two were republished as *Theory and Processes of History* (Berkeley and Los Angeles: University of California Press, 1941). For a bibliography of related writings by Teggart, see the 1977 reprint of *Theory and Processes of History* by the University of California Press.

21. Park developed his thesis in "Human Migration and the Marginal Man," *American Journal of Sociology* (1928), 33:881–93; "Personality and Culture Conflict," *Publications of the American Sociological Society* (1931) 25:95–110; and "Culture Conflict and the Marginal Man," the Introduction to E. V. Stonequist, *The Marginal Man* (New York: Scribner's, 1937), pp. xiii–xvii. The three essays are reprinted in Robert Ezra Park, *Race and Culture* (New York: Free Press, 1950). Park was also drawing on Georg Simmel's characterization of the "stranger."

22. Arnold Toynbee's monumental work is *A Study of History* (12 vols.; London: Oxford University Press, 1934–1961). A concise expression of some of his basic theses appeared in his *Civilization on Trial* (New York: Oxford University Press, 1948). His dependence on Hume is acknowledged in *A Study of History*, 1:468–76, and on Teggart in *Civilization on Trial*, pp. 8–9. Toynbee carefully assessed racial and environmental theories of civilization before offering an alternative; see *A Study of History*, 1:205–71.

23. Theodosius Dobzhansky, *Mankind Evolving* (New Haven: Yale University Press, 1962), p. 17.

24. Alexander Alland, Jr., *Human Diversity* (New York: Columbia University Press, 1971); see esp. pp. 170–76.

25. The rare attempt to approach these requirements has understandably evoked the amused disbelief of social scientists. See the reaction to W. D. Hamilton's effort of S. L. Washburn, "Animal Behavior and Social Anthropology," in Michael S. Gregory, Anita Silvers, and Diane Sutch, eds., *Sociobiology and Human Nature* (San Francisco: Jossey-Bass, 1978), pp. 54–56.

26. François Jacob, "Evolution and Tinkering," *Science* (June 10, 1977), 196:1161–66.

27. The question is put by W. W. Howells, cited in Dobzhansky, *Mankind Evolving*, p. 68.

28. Biologists obviously do observe what they call behavioral flexibility or plasticity in animals. Interesting examples: Michael H. MacRoberts and Barbara R. MacRoberts, *Social Organization and Behavior of the Acorn Woodpecker in Central Coastal California*, Ornithological Monographs no. 21 (Washington: The American Ornithological Union, 1976); Peter B. Stacy and Carl E. Bock, "Social Plasticity in the Acorn Woodpecker," *Science* (1978), 202:1298–1300; Amotz Zahavi, "The Social Behavior of the White Wagtail *Motacilla Alba Alba* Wintering in Israel," *Ibis* (1971), 113:203–11; Laidlaw Williams, "Breeding Behavior of the Brewer Blackbird," *Condor* (1952) 54:3–47; John R. Krebs, Michael H. MacRoberts, and J. M. Cullen, "Flocking and Feeding in the Great Tit *Parus Major*—An Experimental Study," *Ibis* (1972), 114:507–30; Jerram L. Brown, "Alternate Routes to Sociality in Jays—With a Theory for the Evolution of Altruism and Communal Breeding," *American Zoologist* (1974), 14:63–80; M. P. Harris, "Abnormal Migration and Hybridization of *Larus Argentatus* and *L. Fuscus* After Interspecies Fostering Experiments," *Ibis* (1970), 112:488–98; Glen E. Woolfenden, "Florida Scrub Jay Helpers at the Nest," *Auk* (1975), 92:1–15; W. H. Thorpe, *Bird-Song; The Biology of Vocal Communication and Expression in Birds* (Cambridge: Cambridge University Press, 1961); Thelma Rowell, *The Social Behavior of Monkeys* (Middlesex, England: Penguin Books, 1972); Hans Kummer, *Primate Societies: Group Techniques of Ecological Adaptation* (Chicago: Aldine, Atherton, 1971); M. Kawai, "Newly Acquired Pre-cultural Behavior in the Natural Troop of Japanese Monkeys on Koshima Islet," *Primates* (1965), 6:1–30. I am indebted to Barbara R. MacRoberts for most of these references.

6. HUMAN NATURE AND CULTURE

1. Sociologists and anthropologists distinguish between society and culture for certain purposes, but the fact that they are talking about very closely related phenomena is apparent from their frequent use of the term "sociocultural." Since my purpose here is to distinguish both human societies and human cultures from nonhuman, I use the terms in conjunction or interchangeably.

223

2. John Howland Rowe, noting that anthropology is distinguished by its recognition of the scientific importance of physical and cultural differences among human populations, details the appearance of the "perspective distance" necessary for this operation in the Italian Renaissance of the fourteenth and fifteenth centuries. "The Renaissance Foundations of Anthropology," *American Anthropologist* (1965), 67:1–20.

3. The history of this effort is a substantial part of the general history of sociology and anthropology, and it cannot be reviewed here. For an identification of "the social" as the object of sociological study, Émile Durkheim is preeminent. See especially his basic *De la Division du Travail Social* (Paris: Alcan, 1893). For brief and formal statements, see Durkheim, *Les Règles de la Méthode Sociologique* (Paris: Alcan, 1895); and "Cours de Science Sociale: Leçon d'Ouverture," *Revue Internationale de l'Enseignement* (Janvier à Juin 1888), 15:23–48. For a striking demonstration of social influences on individual behavior, Durkheim, *Le Suicide: Étude de Sociologie* (Paris: Alcan, 1897). For a highly technical and painstaking effort to define and distinguish human social action as the subject matter of sociology, see Max Weber, *Economy and Society*, ed. by Guenther Roth and Claus Wittich (Berkeley: University of California Press, 1978), vol. 1, ch. 1. A parallel figure in the history of anthropology is Franz Boas. His formulation of a culture concept is scattered through several writings. For bibliography and a history of Boas's contribution see the excellent analysis by George W. Stocking, Jr., "Franz Boas and the Culture Concept in Historical Perspective," in *Race, Culture, and Evolution* (New York: Free Press, 1968), pp. 195–233. For a more general history of the concept of culture, see A. L. Kroeber and Clyde Kluckhohn, "Culture," *Papers of the Peabody Museum of American Archaeology and Ethnology* (Cambridge, Mass.: Harvard University Press, 1952) vol. 47, no. 1. I try here to get at the meaning of human society and culture by discussing historical interpretations of these phenomena rather than the structural, systematic, and static models that dominate so much of the recent literature. For a discussion on this issue, see Stephen Toulmin, "Rediscovering History," *Encounter* (January 1971), 36:53–64.

4. See David Hume, *Essays: Moral, Political and Literary* (London: Grant Richards, 1903), esp. pp. 202–3, 207–8, 210, 211.

5. James Dunbar, *Essays on the History of Mankind in Rude and Cultivated Ages* (2d ed.; London: 1781), pp. 171, 178, 181.

6. Hugh Murray, *Enquiries Historical and Moral, Respecting the Character of Nations* (Edinburgh: Ballantine, 1808), pp. 36–37, 54. Didactic passages on the social character of human history are few in Murray; but his entire work is an exposition of how the different forms of association among people have different results over time.

7. Theodor Waitz, *Introduction to Anthropology*, ed. from the first volume of *Anthropologie der Naturvolkes* [1858] by J. Frederick Collingwood (London: Longman, Green, Longman, and Roberts, 1863), pp. 7, 344–50, 380.

8. This is not to deny that species other than man might have had *something like* histories in the form of opportunistic activities, as mentioned at the close of chapter 5. It is also not to deny that there has been, and perhaps continues to be, a relationship between events in human evolution and events in human history. Convincing and highly interesting results of work on this relationship are presented in S. L. Washburn, "Speculations on the Interrelations of the History of Tools and Biological Evolution," *Human Biology* (1959), 31:21–31; "Tools and Human Evolution," *Scientific American* (1960), 203:62–75; Jane B. Lancaster, "On the Evolution of Tool-using Behavior," *American Anthropologist* (1968), 70:56–66; K. P. Oakley, "Tools Makyth Man," *Antiquity* (1957), 31:199–209.

9. George Cornewall Lewis, *A Treatise on the Methods of Observation and Reasoning in Politics*, 2 vols. (London: Parker, 1852), 1:51.

10. G. G. Simpson, "The History of Life," in *Evolution after Darwin*, Sol Tax, ed., vol. 1: *The Evolution of Life* (Chicago: University of Chicago Press, 1960), pp. 117–19.

11. George Cornewall Lewis, *An Essay on the Influence of Authority in Matters of Opinion* (London: Longmans, Green, 1875), p. 95.

12. Waitz, *Introduction*, pp. 7–8, 10–11.

13. Jacques Monod, *Chance and Necessity; an Essay on the*

Natural Philosophy of Modern Biology, trans. by Austryn Wainhouse (New York: Vintage Books, 1971), pp. 152–54.

14. The point is noted, parenthetically, by Howard E. Gruber, *Darwin on Man* (New York: Dutton, 1974), p. 97, and by Stephen Jay Gould, *Ever Since Darwin* (New York: Norton, 1977), p. 101. The significance of dated historical materials was more clearly seen by Margaret T. Hodgen, *Early Anthropology in the Sixteenth and Seventeenth Centuries* (Philadelphia: University of Pennsylvania Press, 1964), pp. 452–53.

15. This concern is expressed forcefully by Mary Midgley, *Beast and Man: The Roots of Human Nature* (Ithaca, N.Y.: Cornell University Press, 1978).

16. The point is brought out by Stocking, *Race.* See esp. "Lamarckianism in American Social Science, 1890–1915," pp. 234–69.

17. Frederick J. Teggart, *Theory and Processes of History* (Berkeley: University of California Press, 1977), p. 298.

18. Theodosius Dobzhansky, *Mankind Evolving* (New Haven: Yale University Press, 1962), pp. 74–75. But Dobzhansky also observed that the location of traits differentiating men in the spectrum of genotypic and environmental causes "is known only sketchily or not at all." "The Biological Concept of Heredity as Applied to Man," in *The Nature and Transmission of the Genetic and Cultural Characteristics of Human Populations* (New York: Millbank Memorial Fund, 1957), p. 15.

19. Max Weber recognized the possible relevance of biological factors to human social phenomena, but he also insisted that "all these facts do not discharge sociology from the obligation, in full awareness of the narrow limits to which it is confined, to accomplish what it alone can do." *Economy and Society,* 1:8, 17. Again, when Weber considered the possibility of explaining biologically the appearance of certain types of rationality exclusively in the Occident, he declined following that lead, not on the grounds that the biological factor is irrelevant (he was personally "inclined to think the importance of biological heredity very great"), but because there is a fundamental responsibility to explore all avenues of historical explanation in view of the absence, so far, of requisite biological knowledge. *The Protestant Ethic and the Spirit of Capital-*

ism, trans. by Talcott Parsons (New York: Scribner, 1958), pp. 30–31.

20. A. L. Kroeber, *Anthropology*, new ed., rev. (New York: Harcourt, Brace, 1948), p. 179.

21. Teggart, *Theory and Processes*, pp. 178, 282, 298–300, 303. For another expression of this view see A. L. Kroeber, "Eighteen Professions," *American Anthropologist* (April–June 1915), 17:284–85 (professions 4 and 8).

22. Auguste Comte, *Cours de Philosophie Positive*, 4e ed. (Paris: Baillière 1877), 4:321–23. Attribution of originality to Comte must always be modified, of course, by acknowledgment of his indebtedness to Saint-Simon.

23. These views are scattered through the writings of Marx and Engels, but for specific observations see: Karl Marx, *Capital: A Critique of Political Economy*, vol. 1, *The Process of Capitalist Production*, trans. by Samuel Moore and Edward Aveling, ed. by Frederick Engels (Chicago: Charles H. Kerr, 1906), p. 198; Karl Marx and Friedrich Engels, *The German Ideology*, parts 1 and 3, R. Pascal, ed. (New York: International Publishers, 1939), pp. 7, 74, 76; Friedrich Engels, *Dialectics of Nature*, trans. and ed. by Clemens Dutt (New York: International Publishers, 1960), ch. 9, "The Part Played by Labour in the Transition from Ape to Man." Marx presented a concrete case of human history-making shaped by circumstances in his *Eighteenth Brumaire of Louis Napoleon*. Lia Formigari notes the strong antecedents of these views of Marx and Engels in the writings of Lord Monboddo. She points out the common assumption that underlay anthropology prior to the formulation of a historical concept of culture: "the presupposition of the existence of a natural individual who is not a product of history but rather history's point of departure." "Language and Society in the Late Eighteenth Century," *Journal of the History of Ideas* (1974), 35:275–92. For another expression of the Marxist idea that man makes his own history, see V. Gordon Childe, *Man Makes Himself* (London: Watts, 1936).

24. Émile Durkheim's most eloquent statement of these views appears in his "The Dualism of Human Nature and its Social Conditions," [1914], trans. by Charles Blend and most recently reprinted in *Émile Durkheim on Morality and Society*,

227

Robert Bellah, ed. (Chicago: University of Chicago Press, 1973), p. 150. See also his "Introduction à la morale," *Revue Philosophique* (Janvier à Décembre 1920), 89–90:81–97, for a forceful description of human existence as historical existence.

25. Stocking, *Race*, ch. 9.

26. Clifford Geertz, *The Interpretation of Cultures; Selected Essays* (New York: Basic Books, 1973), pp. 49, 52–53.

27. José Ortega y Gasset, *History as a System, and other Essays Toward a Philosophy of History* (New York: Norton, 1961), p. 217.

28. See Konrad Lorenz, *On Aggression*, trans. by Marjorie Kerr Wilson (New York: Bantam Books, 1967), p. 251; C. D. Darlington, *The Facts of Life* (London: Allen & Unwin, 1953).

29. Dobzhansky, *Mankind Evolving*, p. 18.

30. A. L. Kroeber, *The Nature of Culture* (Chicago: University of Chicago Press, 1952), p. 22. The remark appears in a prefatory note to his famous essay, "The Superorganic" (1917), reprinted in this volume.

7. ACTIVITY AND BEHAVIOR

1. "Activity" and "behavior" are used here for purposes different from Weber's when he sought to distinguish human actions as understandable in terms of the subjective meanings attached to them by actors. Weber argued that we cannot understand the behavior of nonhuman animals because we do not have satisfactory access to their subjective states of mind. He therefore questioned the appropriateness of seeking an understanding of human social action through observation of other social animals. See Max Weber, *Economy and Society*, Guenther Roth and Claus Wittich, eds. (Berkeley: University of California Press, 1978), 1:4–24. This Weberian distinction has been used in a most interesting fashion by Vernon Reynolds, *The Biology of Human Action* (San Francisco: Freeman, 1976), to point out weaknesses in theories of human social action that are based upon studies of other animals.

2. Conditions of innovative action are dealt with here in terms of individuals within a society and of whole societies. It is necessary to bear in mind, of course, that within any given society classes, castes, age grades, sexes, and groups of other

kinds differ greatly in the extent to which they are shielded from or exposed to disruptive, innovative, or liberating influences.

3. Herbert Spencer, "A Theory of Population," *Westminster Review* (April 1852), n.s., 1:468–501. For a quite sympathetic review of "selectionist" social theory, see Pitirim Sorokin, *Contemporary Sociological Theories* (New York: Harper, 1928), ch. 5.

4. As Washburn has remarked "evolution is a magic word" in such discussions. S. L. Washburn, communication in *American Psychologist* (May 1976), 31:353–55.

INDEX

Activity, 179–98 *passim;* defined, 5, 185; opportunistic, in animals, 121, 147–48, 225 n8; and historical change, 158–59; *see also* Behavior

Adaptation, 4, 80, 81, 84, 93; relation of cultural and organic, 73, 76–77, 113–14, 120–21, 146–47, 189, 192, 212 n21, 219–20 n43

Agassiz, Alexander, 221 n8

Aggression, 64, 67, 76, 105, 186, 187, 212 n24; sociobiological explanation of, 70, 72–73, 81, 116, 117, 118, 165

Albertus Magnus, 10

Alexander, Richard D., 209 n6

Alland, Alexander, Jr., 141, 168

Altruism, 67, 165, 208 n35; sociobiological explanations of, 64, 70, 118, 120, 210 n9

Analogy, 12, 24, 38, 55, 75, 112, 149, 200–201 n12

Angels, 8, 10, 12, 14, 88, 104

Animal–man comparisons, 3, 7, 11, 13, 14, 15, 18–19, 27, 28, 31, 32, 74, 104, 107, 120, 148, 149, 156, 159, 163, 167, 169, 172, 184, 185, 186, 203 n40, 206 n19, 207 n28, 228 n1

Animals, 2, 44, 57, 64, 65, 95, 101, 121, 182–83, 188–89, 198, 204 n51; in ancient thought, 9, 12, 14, 19; in medieval thought, 10, 13; as moral guides, 9, 26; communication among, 31; human kinship with, 3, 8, 9, 14, 17, 28, 29, 33, 34, 59, 119–20; humans different from, 4, 6, 153, 166, 171; humans inferior to, 26, 30; societies among, 5, 22, 149, 157, 158; opportunistic activities among, 147–48, 225 n8; apes, 8, 10, 13, 14, 16, 18–19, 21, 22, 31, 43, 47, 107, 168, 201 n15, 203 n40; baboons, 10, 21, 22, 149; chimpanzees, 13, 74, 188; monkeys, 18, 21, 22, 163, 188; orangutans, 13,

231

INDEX

Sociology, *see* Humanistic studies; Social sciences
Sorokin, Pitirim, 208 n2
Soul, 15, 16, 27, 30, 31, 49, 94, 214 n37
Spate, O. H. K., 214 n2
Speech, *see* Language
Spencer, Herbert, 12, 113, 192, 193, 207 n32
Spencer, Theodore, 29
Stacy, Peter B., 223 n28
Stocking, George W., Jr., 172, 224 n3, 226 n16
Stonequist, E. V., 222 n21
Superorganic, 66, 177; *see also* Culture, independent reality of

Teggart, Frederick J., 139, 140, 142, 143, 156, 167–68, 172; active and inactive peoples, 135; and cultural differences, 135; theory of change, 135–38; comparison of histories, 136; man "as given," 169, 227 n21
Theriophily, 26, 203 n46
Thorpe, W. H., 223 n28
Thucydides, 42
Tillyard, E. M. W., 13
Tools, 107, 174, 175, 194, 195
Toulmin, Stephen, 224 n3
Toynbee, A. J., 156, 172; and cultural differences, 139–41, 222 n22
Tradition: as control of behavior, 5, 57, 152, 154, 156–57, 185, 189, 190, 191, 196; as transmission of culture, 114; as persistence, 124, 131, 135, 139; and biological mechanisms, 146–47
Trivers, Robert, 84, 209 n6
Turgot, A., 99
Tylor, Edward Burnett, 41, 46, 49, 53, 54
Tyson, Edward, 13–14, 22

Uniformitarianism, 98, 110, 132, 215 n4
Unity of nature, 6, 9, 32, 75, 96, 97–98, 142, 147, 165, 183, 184
Universal process: of natural selection, 6, 32; of human history, 42, 94, 100–101, 106, 111; as locus of the natural, 99; and sociobiology, 115, 119, 122; *see also* Cultural similarities; Unity of nature

Valleroy, L. A., 211 n18
Van den Berghe, P. L., 211 n18
Vercors [Bruller, Jean], 202 n31

Waitz, Theodor, 57, 133, 140, 142, 143, 154–56, 172; and cultural differences, 128–29, 132, 155, 164; and race theory, 128–29, 130, 132, 155; and change, 129, 130, 131
Washburn, S. L., 222 n25, 225 n8, 229 n4
Weber, Max, 38, 168; and relevance of biology, 226 n19; distinction between action and behavior, 228 n1
West-Eberhard, M. J., 209 n6
Westermarck, Edward, 210 n10
Wilberforce, Bishop Samuel, 49
Wild men, 10, 11, 13, 16, 20, 23
Williams, Laidlaw, 223 n28
Wilson, Edward O.: on aim of sociobiology, 62–63; on genetic basis of behavior, 63, 68–70, 71–72, 74–75, 116, 163; on sociobiology and the social sciences, 64; on repertory of human behaviors, 64; on natural selection, 65, 143; on a scientific ethic, 65–66, 88; on denial of social and cultural